THE DEAD SEA SCROLLS AND THE ROOTS OF CHRISTIANITY AND ISLAM:

RE-ERECTING THE FALLEN TENT OF DAVID IN THE LAND NORTH OF DAMASCUS

ROBERT EISENMAN

The Dead Sea Scrolls and the Roots of Christianity and Islam: Re-Erecting the Fallen Tent of David in the Land North of Damascus

The Way Publishing

ISBN: 978-1793314710
In Publication Data
Eisenman, Robert

TABLE of CONTENTS

PREFACE

The subjects in this monograph to some extent are in the author's two 1,000-page books *James the Brother of Jesus: The Key to Unlocking the Secrets of Early Christianity and the Dead Sea Scrolls,* Penguin, *1997–98* and *The New Testament Code: The Cup of the Lord, the Damascus Covenant, and the Blood of* Christ, Watkins/Sterling, 2006; and in his collection of essays: *The Dead Sea Scrolls and the First Christians,* Harper-Collins, 2004. However we have never dealt with these two key technical problems concerning Jewish sects and the issues raised in some of the central delineations by the contemporary First-Century Jewish Historian Josephus in the manner that we have written them here.

The issues are very simple and central to a true delineation of the period. First of all, Josephus was himself working from sources, almost none of which have survived except through the prism of his and others' references—two of whom are Strabo of Cappodocea and Nicolaus of Damascus, an Herodian diplomat in Rome in the First Century BCE. But Josephus, who was born in the late Thirties CE, was not a mature observer until the last days of the Jewish Commonweal, just prior to the destruction of the Temple and the Fall of Jerusalem in 70 CE, at which point—seemingly "to save his own skin"—he went over to the Romans, proclaimed their future Emperor Vespasian, the Roman Commander in Palestine at the time, "the Messiah" or 'World Ruler who was to come out of Palestine" (the same "Prophecy" early Christians were applying to their "Jesus" and the Dead Sea Scrolls were applying to their expected "Leader"), was adopted into the Imperial Family itself—therefore his cognomen "Flavius", the Imperial Name of that family—and was, in effect, the Traitor of all traitors.

So his work must be read circumspectly or through a prism as it were, to correct—just as we have to correct telescopes out in space—not only for his point-of-view, but also for his errors or own misunderstandings of his sources. This is why his "Confusions of Pharisees and Essenes", two of the key then-extant Parties he identifies—not to mention "Pharisees and Zealots" and "Zealots and Essenes"—are so important. This is what he had done in as succinct a manner possible in the article by said title. The point is that you cannot understand the period Leading up to "Jesus" and the birth of "Christianity," as it were, without understanding these sorts of fine points.

When Josephus is using the word "Pharisee", sometimes he means it in a generic sense, based on the original Hebrew meaning "to split away from" and, therefore, simply "sectarian"; or, as is sometimes the case, "Essene." This is particularly the case when he says that Herod (c. 55 BCE–4 BCE) "thought greater of the Essenes than their mortal nature deserved." The group he is really talking about here are "the Pharisees"—who later survive the destruction of the Temple and go on to create the Rabbinic Judaism, we all speak se familiarly about today.

He cannot mean "Essenes" because it is certainly clear that he destroyed their settlement by the Dead Sea in the 30s–20s BCE Period—this according to the archaeological on-site evidence we have now uncovered; nor, if the literature found at this settlement (known in the field as "Qumran" after the Arabic name for the locale)—which is commonly designated by scholars as "Essene"—is any guide, then that literature has to be seen as distinctly anti Herod, anti-Herodian, and anti-foreign control in Jerusalem an(Palestine generally.

The same can be said for "the *Zaddik*-idea" as per the name of the article by that name. This must be understood in order to know who the third "Party" identified by Josephus might be, i.e., "the (Sadducees," and what their relation is both to Qumran and "the Priesthood" being promoted there and, one might say, by the late "Christianity" of the Letter to the Hebrews in "the

Priesthood after the Order of Melchizedek" generally (i.e., in both Arabic and Hebrew a "Righteous King").

What he demonstrates in his works, particularly *Maccabees, Zadokites, Christians and Qumran: A New Hypothesis of Qumran Origins* collected in *The Dead Sea Scrolls and the First Christians* above, is that there were two—perhaps even three —groups of so-called "Sadducees": one before Herod, one after him, and one at Qumran; and the last one—the one at Qumran—had an esoteric interpretation of these things as did the Christianity" of the New Testament to come. But there all semblance ceases as the "Essene" or "Zealot" literature at Qumran; apocalyptic, xenophobic, militant, law-oriented, aggressive and unaccommodating, and intolerant. This is unlike the manner in which "Christianity," as we know it, promotes itself even though some of these strains are clearly identifiable underlying some of the portraits of its "Jesus", albeit overlaid by more antinomian, pacifistic', compromising, and accommodating material its editors wished to include.

That is why "the *Zaddik*-Idea and the Zadokite Priesthood" is so important as we have delineated it here. Since the Dead Sea Scrolls ill their Leadership cadre "the Sons of Zadok", i.e., these are *Saddukim*" or "Sadducees," as the transliteration into Greek would me it; then to understand that this is not necessarily a genealogical :notation, but rather one of "Keepers of the Covenant" or "the Law' ("the *Torat* of Moses" as it were in Islamic terms), as it is put elsewhere, and therefore an esoteric understanding, leading up to the ore antinomian esoteric understanding of its 'Priesthood" in Christianity as we have come to know it, is crucial for understanding these matters. In other words, an understanding of he *Zaddik*-idea" of the Qumran conception of its "Righteous Priesthood is the very basis of coming to terms with the new theological approach of these hitherto own and tremendously important documents.

We have done it for the first time, fully and completely, in this monograph. Such an understanding, too, leads into a direct appreciation of how James "the brother of Jesus," as he is delineated in early Church literature—himself also and always called, like "the Righteous Teacher" of the Qumran literature, "James the Just"/"James the Righteous One"/or "James the *Zaddik*"—could have gone into the Inner Sanctum of the Temple by himself and done an atonement on behalf of the whole People, for which he seems to have been executed by his Establishment and Herodian ideological opponents. It also makes it clear that what we have at Qumran are not just ordinary "Sadducees" of the later Herodian Period and New Testament delineation; but rather "Messianic Sadducees", their total opposite and reverse factional categorization—or as some might have it "Essenes" or "Zealots" or "Zealot Essenes."

Professor Dr. Robert Eisenman
California State University, Long Beach USA

Visiting Scholar
Center for Civilisational Dialogue
University Malaya
23 February–20 March 2010

CONFUSIONS OF PHARISEES AND ESSENES IN JOSEPHUS

Several historiographic and textual problems emerge from identifying the Community at Qumran with "the Essenes." Since most of our knowledge about "Essenes" is based on notices in Josephus, it is reasonable to suppose that some of these difficulties stem from Josephus' own confusions and distortions or purposeful obfuscations of data. In this regard, it is often overlooked that Josephus was himself working from sources—two of the most well known of which he admits to using were Strabo of Cappadocia and Vicolaus of Damascus.

In our first published work on this subject *Maccabees, Zadokites, Christians and Qumran*, we delineated two groups of Sadducees, me "Opposition" and the other "Establishment." The latter, for the sake of convenience, we designated "Boethusian." This split is reflected in both Talmudic and Karaite sources in allusion to a split between "Zadok and Boethus." In this work, too, we also documented a parallel earlier "split" between "Opposition" and Establishment Hassidaeans," i.e., those "Hassidaeans" whom 2 Macc. 14:5 labels "war-mongers, anxious to foment sedition", and another more temporizing group which goes over to Alcirnus (a High Priest of questionable lineage appointed by the Syrians). The former group, again for the sake of convenience, we labeled Zadokite Hassidaean" as opposed to the latter, "Pharisee Hassidaean."

Both splits, the first in "the Hassidaean Movement" and the second in "the Sadduceean", have to do with attitudes towards foreigners generally and, in particular as already signaled, foreign appointment of high priests. One should realize that in these splits and confusions one has the origins of Second Temple Party and/or "Sectarian" affiliations and strife. In fact, these terminologies have tended to slide around quite a good deal depending on who was using them and how, and nowhere is this lack of precision more evident than in the works of Josephus.

A proper understanding of the attitude of Qumran towards the Herodian Establishment is also essential in approaching these problems. Many scholars have found it impossible to determine whether Qumran was pro-Herodian or anti-Herodian and, therefore, have been unable to make any real sense of the relative abandonment of the settlement during Herod's reign. The crucial material relative to Qumran's attitude towards the Herodian Establishment comes in the Damascus Document, in particular, in the condemnation of "fornication" and "riches" found in Columns IV–VI and elsewhere (and actually paralleled in other documents like the Temple Scroll)—even though this document has often been placed by many on paleographic grounds in the Second Century BCE. I strenuously criticized such placement on these sorts of grounds, preferring "the internal evidence" or what the documents themselves said, instead.

In these columns and in documents like the Temple Scroll, by "fornication" *(zanut,* Qumran understands both "marriage with nieces" and "divorce"—practices absolutely characteristic of the Herodian Establishment in the First Century and, not accidentally, they are also at the bottom of this Establishment's difficulties with so-called "Zealots" and/or early "Christians." "Riches" is, of course, another leitmotif of the Herodian Priestly Establishment and underpins the basis Josephus' descriptions of most "Herodian" High Priestly clans, not to mention the Herodian family itself which stole just about everything it could get its hands on. The third charge made in the "Three Nets of Belial" section of the Damascus Document, "idolatry", is beyond the scope of this essay but it is easily elucidated within this framework.

When Herod came to power, he despoiled the previous aristocracy and bribed the famous Mark Anthony to behead the last Maccabean Priest-King Antigonus "for otherwise," as he says, "the Jews could in no way be pacified." He had all the members of their previous Sanhedrin, except for two he names as "Pollio and Sameas" (probably the Rabbinic "Pair" Hillel and Shammai—though some say Abtalion and Shamaiah if they can in fact be distinguished) liquidated, many of whom had previously wished to condemn him For executing the 'nationalist' "bandit" chief Hezekiah.

As Josephus portrays Nerod, though he promoted "such men of the private men of the city as had been of his party, he never left off avenging and punishing every day those that had chosen to be of he party of his enemies." Where "Pollio the Pharisee and Sameas, a Disciple of his," were concerned, Josephus unequivocally tells us hat Herod "honored them above all the rest, for when Jerusalem was besieged by the Roman General Sossius and Herod (c. 37 BCE), hey advised the citizens to open the gates to Herod."

Pollio's advice and Sameas' recognition of Herod's leadership potential (the Herod he characterizes as "an admirable man") should be seen as paradigmatic for the political conduct of those whom we would define as and now call "Pharisees" and those whom Qumran, apparently lumping several of these Establishment groups together, refers to as "Seekers after Smooth Things" according to our definition, "those seeking accommodation with foreigners" in this context and in *MZCQ*). It epitomizes Pharisaic political conduct from the time of Alexander Jannaeus and the Demetrius affair (late Second Century BCE and, as we shall see, even before) to that of R. Yohanan b. Zacchai at the time of the fall of the 'Temple in 70 CE, not to mention two other self-professed Pharisees", Paul and Josephus. Just before the Temple was going to ill, the Talmud portrays R. Yohanan as "having an arrow shot into the

Emperor's camp to tell him he was one of the Emperor's friends" or Paul's "Establishment" sensibilities, no better picture could be found than Romans 13.1–7.

For perhaps the best picture of the *modus operandi* of this Herodian, Pharisaic, and "Boethusian Sadduceean" alliance, see War 2.17.3f., where "the Men of Power" (i.e., "the Herodians"), the High Priests (i.e., our "Boethusian Sadducees"), and the principal men of the Pharisees try to convince those whom Josephus persistently calls "the Innovators" (i.e., those who wished ideological and institutional change) that their forefathers had accepted gifts and sacrifices from foreigners (here, of course, is the basis of the "idolatry" charge leveled against the Jerusalem Establishment at Qumran).

Failing this and "perceiving that the sedition was too far gone for them to subdue", it is this combination of Establishment groups that actually sent for the Romans—as their precursors in the time of Alexander Jannaeus and, before him, Judas Maccabee—had the Greeks, "to come with an army to the city and cut off the sedition." One should note here that one of the intermediaries for this process was an Herodian collaborator and family member named, Josephus distinctly names as "Saulos"—the same name, of course, as "Paul" in the New Testament.

Whether Pollio and Sameas are "Hillel and Shamnai" or "Abtalion and Shemaiah", or a combination of both (Josephus obviously considers them well known) is immaterial for our purposes. In the earliest of these kinds of notices about so-called Pharisees, where Josephus describes in the Hezekiah affair how Sameas recognized Herod's leadership potential, Josephus notes how Sameas alone of all the members of the Sanhedrin of that time survived and tells how he "was greatly honored, . . . because when the city was afterwards besieged by Herod and Sossius, he persuaded the people to admit Herod into it." In addition to not clearly distinguishing between "Essenes" and "Pharisees!" in these notices, Josephus confuses Sameas and Pollio with each other.

In the later notice about the latter, probably from a different source than this earlier one, it is "Pollio, who at the time when Herod was once upon his trial of life or death, foretold by way of reproach. . .how this Herod. . . would afterward punish them all, which had its completion in time." One should note in all these notices about "Pharisees," the general orientation of seeking accommodation with foreigners (among whom, I would include "Herodians") and the persistent theme of fortune-telling.

If one now turns to Josephus' references to the group he refers to as "Essenes", one encounters similar themes. Josephus first mentions "Essenes" in relation to someone he calls "Judas" in the period of the end of John Hyrcanus' reign (c. 100 BCE). He describes this man as "a prophet" frequenting the Temple precincts "with companions and friends who abode with him as scholars *in order to learn the art of foretelling things to come*" and "*who never missed the truth in his predictions*" (italics mine). The "prophesying" or "soothsaying" theme is paradigmatic.

Like Sameas, Pollio the Pharisee, Menachem the Essene, Simeon the Essene, Yohanan ben Zacchai, and Josephus himself (not to mention Acts' picture of "*the teachers and prophets*" of Paul's Antioch Community—italics mine); Judas supposedly predicts the imminent demise of John Hyrcanus' son Antigonus at the hands of his older brother Aristobulus (a man Josephus designates as the first Hasmonaean "King"). Aristobdus, who is portrayed as dying an excruciating death because of this crime, even though he had already repented of it, is then succeeded by his anti-Pharisaic third brother, Alexander Jannaeus. One should note that the story whose source, as in the later Sameas material, appears to be Strabo of Cappadocea is generally hostile to Maccabean Kingly pretensions just as the Pharisees were presented as hostile to John Hyrcanus' High-Priestly pretensions earlier.

The next reference to "Essenes" comes side-by-side with Josephus' second reference to Pollio and Sameas. It follows Josephus' description of Herod's police tactics and the people's consequent hostility towards him, including a remark about Herod's) own introduction of "innovations (a word Josephus usually reserves, is we have seen, for the practices of the Seditionists or Revolutionaries) to the dissolution of their religion and the disuse of their own customs." In an attempt to overcome the people's hostility, Herod remitted a third of their taxes and introduced a loyalty oath, but "those who could not be induced to acquiesce to his scheme of government he persecuted in all manner of ways."

In parallel though non-correlating notices, he describes both "the Essenes" and "Pollio, Sameas, and their company" as being excused from the oath in spite of the harsh repression just noted. Pollio and Sameas are described as keeping the company of a large group of "scholars" in exactly the manner that Judas "of the sect of Essenes" had been described as being accompanied by "companions and friends who abode with him as scholars" earlier (italics mine).

In the very next sentence, after noting how Herod excused "the Essenes", as he had the Company of Pollio and Sameas, from swearing their loyalty (obviously out of regard for the ample evidence he already had of their loyalty), Josephus goes on to describe the former as a sect living "the same kind of life as those the Greeks call Pythagoraeans", by which he again appears to be alluding to the camaraderie of scholars, just described in regard to "Judas the Essene" and both "Pollio the Pharisee and Sameas." We conclude that, at this point Josephus is confusing overlapping materials from different sources using slightly differing terminologies—perhaps from the separate accounts of Strabo of Cappadocea and Nicolaus of Damascus noted earlier—but which he has, at least, the perspicuity to realize typologically belong together.

Josephus' next reference to "Essenes" follows almost immediately. The confusions and evidence of parallel non-correlating sources continue. In this testimony, Josephus tries to explain why Herod "held the Essenes in such honor." As in his "Judas of the sect of the Essenes" story, the folkloric aspects of the presentation are fairly patent. He tells a story about "one of these Essenes whose name was Menachem" (later the name of someone who seems to he a grandson of Judas the Galielean). Describing him in terms evocative of those he used to describe Sameas, whom he called '*Righteous*', he says Menachem "conducted his life in an excellent manner." For this story, anyhow, it seems the reason Herod held "the Essenes" in such high esteem was that, when he (Herod) was a schoolboy, Menachem saluted him as king and when Herod protested, Menachem smacked him on the bottom. But this of course is nothing but a variation on the story of Sameas the Pharisee above.

This theme of predicting the future—what by this time goes by the name of "prophesying"—or having "God-given knowledge of future events" is common to all these episodes. The only difference is that Sameas predicted Herod's future kingship when Herod was already a young man; Menachem, when he was still a young boy. As Sameas refers to Herod as "an excellent man", so Menachem describes him "found worthy by God" and, at a later point, even predicts an exceedingly long reign for him, at which "Herod. . . gave Menachem his hand and. . . from that time on, continued to honor all Essenes."

The policy of flattering alien or foreign-imposed local rulers with prophecies of future greatness or longevity was typical of Pharisaic practice from the time of Sameas or Pollio (or both) until that of the fall of the Temple, when either Josephus or R. Yohanan b. Zacchai, both self-professed Pharisees, have the audacity to apply the "Messianic Prophecy" (i.e., "the Star Prophecy" of Numbers 24:16–17 to Vespasian. In an unguarded moment during his discussion of Vespasian's "Messianic" qualifications at the end of the War, Josephus also inadvertently revealed that this same Messianic "Star Prophecy" was the moving force behind the Uprising against Rome.

That it was held in particularly high esteem in the documents found at Qumran is borne out by reference to it at least three times in the extant corpus—once in the War Scroll, once in the Damascus Document, and once in one of the collection of "Messianict' proof texts known as the "*Testimonia*." In spite of the palpable hostility of "the Essenes" at Qumran to "law-breakers" (including presumably foreigners) and everything the Herodians stood for (e.g., niece marriage, which for them was a matter of family policy, "riches", etc.), not to mention Josephus' indications in conjunction with his testimonies about Essenes of "spies set everywhere" and "many brought to the citadel Hyrcania (near Qumran) both openly and secretly and there put to death"; many scholars persist in believing Josephus' stories about 'toadying' soothsayers where Herod's regard for "the Essenes" is the issue.

At the same, time they attribute the destruction by fire of 'the Essene settlement at Qumran' and its relative abandonment through most of Herod's reign, to an earthquake!

As opposed to this view, whatever the "Essenes" were, it must be understood they were never sycophantic, neither in Josephus nor at Qumran.

Josephus gives incontestable evidence of this, particularly in his description of the unwillingness of the Essenes to blaspheme the Law-Giver (parallel to his description of the "Zealot" unwillingness to "call any man Lord") and their heroic resistance in the war against Rome. As a turncoat and an interrogator of prisoners, if anyone was in a position to know, he was. The "Essene" contempt for "Riches", which forms a large part of this description and is at the bottom of Qumran and Judeo-Christian "Poor" designations, gives further evidence of this.

For its part, Qumran is never obsequious but, rather, always apocalyptic and could never have countenanced the application of "the Messianic Prophecy" to either Romans or Herodians.

Let us now apply our theory of terminological confusions between "Pharisees" and "Essenes" to several well-known examples. In the *Antiquities*, Josephus tells us about one "Sadduk a Pharisee", a leader of those he accuses of "Innovation" and, along with Hezekiah's son Judas the Galilean, a founder of the so-called "Fourth Philosophy" (a "Philosophy" most designate simply as "Zealot"—though Josephus never uses the term until much later—but which I would also call "Messianic"). He describes his doctrines and those of his followers as being like the Pharisees in all things except that they had "an inviolable attachment to liberty", "would not call any man Lord"; and opposed Joezer b. Boethus on the tax issue (i.e., the son of Herod's Sadduceean High Priest imported from Egypt—*n.b.,* the *sitz-im-leben* of "Zadok"/"Boethus" split here). Keeping in mind our designation in *MZCQ* of two Hassidaean groups, one "Pharisaic" and the other "Zadokite", and substituting the terminology "Essene" for "Pharisee" here; the notice would then read "Sadduk an Essene. . .who was in all things like the Pharisees, except he had an inviolable attachment to liberty. . .", etc., etc., which adds considerable terminological precision to the delineation of these groups.

In the reign of Herod's son Archelaus, Josephus tells us about another fortune-telling "man of the sect of Essenes" named Simon (*n.b.,* a favorite name in New Testament presentation), who predicted Archelaus' demise on the basis of a Joseph-like and, on that basis, probably mythological dream about ears of corn. Not without interest, the Slavonic Josephus now refers to this Simon as a "Sadducee." Not only is the constant reiteration of the phraseology "sect of Essenes" interesting (Josephus only uses the term "Essene" as a cognomen later when referring to "John the Essene", a military commander in the early stages of the Uprising); but regardless of one's opinion of the merit of the Slavonic, we can also offer a plausible explanation on the basis of our theory for why a given "Simon" could be thought of as an "Essene" in one account and a "Sadducee" in another. Here, of course, we have confusions of "Sadducees" and "Pharisees."

Even more interesting, the Slavonic Josephus refers to another Establishment-type "scribe of Essene origins", also called "Simon" and closely allied to the son of Herod, we already referred to above, called Archelaus. When the John the Baptist-like "Wild Man" who came in "the way of the Law" and preached revolution (whom the Slavonic also places in the time of Archelaus) is brought before Archelaus, this "Simon" abuses him verbally and assaults But in this instance it is "the Wild Man" who is the "Essene" and Simon the "Pharisee." Our exposition of confusions between Pharisees and Essenes goes a long way towards illuminating this scene as well. The "Man", obviously intended as a simile of John the Baptist (though here unnamed), is correctly portrayed as anti-Herodian; the "scribe of Essene origins named Simon" (possibly equivalent to several illustrious Pharisees in this period by that name including the famous "Shammai"—our "Sameas" above), pro-Herodian.

He is an important Pharisee, as his intimacy with Archelaus conspicuously confirms. Even according to Josephus' detailed exposition of "Essene" customs, he cannot be an "Essene" by any stretch of the imagination, most certainly not a Qumran "Essene." Even more than the example of the "Sadducee" Simon above, it is difficult to dismiss such complex notices, which make 'errors' characteristic of the period we are considering and not the Middle Ages, simply as the products of medieval copyists' errors or inventions. This is true, particularly when they are also at odds with the overt sense of Gospel testimony and, historically speaking, such good sense can be made out of them, however bizarre they may at first appear.

Finally, let us apply this understanding of confusions between "Essene" and "Pharisee" terminologies to the contradictory testimonies about the birth of and nature of the "Hassidaean" Movement in 1 Maccabees and 2 Maccabees, a subject we have discussed at length in *MZCQ*. In the latter, "the Hassidaeans" are portrayed as the supporters of Judas Maccabee par excellence; in the former, as back-sliding defectors who betray him. Substituting the new terminology "Pharisee" (or even proto-Pharisee) for the latter group adds considerable depth and clarity to the portrayal.

When one appreciates that there were two groups descended from the Hassidaeans, one revolutionary and the other "break-away" and accommodating that "split" (the Hebrew basis of the term "Pharisee") over the issue of election or foreign appointment of High Priests; one can understand how one or the other of these groups could in some sources pass for "Essenes" and in others, "Pharisees." According to our view, what 1 Maccabees, in particular, has conserved in its portrait of "the split" between Judas and these "break-away", back-sliding "Hassidaeans" is the birth moment of the Pharisee Party not the Hassidaean.

As the split between those opposed to and those willing to live with foreign intervention continued into the "Herodian Period", if one keeps one's eyes fixed firmly on the anti-Herodian strain of such opposition "Essene" groups and the pro-Herodian strain of Establishment "Pharisee" groups (including so-called "Sadducees" or "Boethusian" Sadducees, whom, as Josephus testifies, were dominated in their post-Herodian embodiment by the Pharisees; one will never go far astray. Here, Qumran's application of the terminology "Seekers after Smooth Things" to the latter orientation is perhaps closer to the mark than any more-modern appreciations of the group this euphemism is generally held to approximate.

THE ZADDIK-IDEA AND THE ZADOKITE PRIESTHOOD

The *Zaddik*-idea, known chiefly in connection with Kabbalah, is found in various parts of the Old Testament. It is also to be found in Qumran literature, Apocrypha and Pseudepigrapha, and theological speculation centering about the Messiah in the New Testament. It takes its origins from several notices concerning it in Genesis relating to two escape and salvation-episodes, that of Noah and Lot. In the first Noah is identified as an "*Ish-Zaddik*" or "Righteous Man" (Gen. 6:9). The context is such that one is comparing the survival of "the Righteous" to the destruction of "the Wicked," i.e., the *Zaddikim* vs. the *Resha'im*, a dichotomy familiar to students of Qumran. Noah is seen by God as "Righteous in his generation." His "Righteousness" is understood as being synonymous with doing "all that the Lord commanded him to do" (7:1 and 6:22—italics mine, the "to do" being particularly important in Qumran ideology and the basis of the word "works", the importance of which we shall see below).

After Noah's miraculous salvation from the flood, a sacrifice is made and a Covenant ratified (we are here not interested in the textual provenance of one or the other of the promises made according to the modem Biblical approach of form and text criticism, since what is under consideration is how Noah was perceived by later generations, not how, when, and why this perception originated). Aside from being instructed to be fruitful, multiply, and people the earth (i.e., with Zaddikim), the ban on the consumption of meat, which in theory must be seen as having been operative since the days of creation, is lifted—albeit to later eyes in a manner that might have only seemed temporary—and the stricture to abstain from blood (so zealously discussed in Paul's communications with James' Jerusalem Church in the matter of the conversion of Gentiles in Acts and 1 Corinthians and still a matter of concern to Jews and Muslims) is imposed.

It is important to understand that from the inception of *"the Zaddik"* terminology, certain Priestly prerogatives adhered to it, i.e., in effect Noah was the first High Priest. That he was "Righteous" as well was an additional factor in his favor. It is his sacrifice and subsequent Covenant with God that, thereafter, opens the way for the consumption of meat on a vast scale. The concomitant to this proposition to the Second Temple mind (the sources relating to it from the First Temple are not extensive enough to make any observations) must have been that, when the sacrifice was no longer operative or it was being carried out by men who were polluted or discredited in some manner—discredited not so much in a genealogical sense but in a moral one—this special Noahic dispensation to consume meat was no longer operative. Thus, the vegetarianism of such individuals as Judas Maccabee and John the Baptist, which has rather often been mistaken in the popular mind with a sort of Hellenistic asceticism. The reasoning processes here are similar to Paul's presentation of Abraham (another of the *Zaddikirn* "called by name", who is vouchsafed the privilege of sacrificing as if he were a Priest)—to say nothing of Muhammad to the same effect—as having come before the Law and therefore not subject to it, whose "faith" rather "counted for him as Righteousness" or, in Paul's tendentious alteration of the sense of that term, combining it with Isaiah 53:11–12, "justified him" or "made him Righteous."

The Lot episode simply serves to reinforce the essentiality of *"the Zaddik"* in the scheme of creation and his soteriological force as embodied in his own ability to survive. Proclaiming that Abraham has commanded his children to "keep the Way of the Lord", "to do Righteousness and Justice" (again, the "doing" motif so important to Qumran and the Letter of James), the text poses the basic question, "will you also destroy the Righteous with the Wicked *(Zaddik im-Rasha ')?*" (Gen. 19:24–33). This theme is reiterated in the bargaining that ensues, until it is decided for the sake of "ten Just Men"—*"the ten Zaddikim"*—God would withhold destruction from the city. For a literalist, as the Second Temple exegete most certainly was, this is a very important conception. Thus, the *Zaddikim* are, not only those who are saved themselves, but also those who bring salvation to others.

As the notion of Resurrection of the Dead developed in the Second Temple Period, probably from a literalist understanding of Ezekiel's vivid similes, it became a self-evident truism that the Resurrection, when it came, would be of "the Just" or "Righteous Ones", and that those from among the living who would escape the final cataclysmic destruction of all the Evil Ones in the manner of Noah and Lot (also pictured in the Koran) and, therefore, enter into the Messianic Kingdom, would be the *Zaddikim.* "These", in the language of Column IV of the Damascus Document, "are *the Sons of Zadok* who will *stand on the Last Days"* (italics mine—note, the deliberate eschatological motif here). The *Zaddik* in his embodiment of Righteous Priest or, as we shall see, "Son of Zadok" would be the one whose confession of sins on behalf of the whole people in the Temple on *Yom Kippur* would alone be efficacious or of soteriological effect. In his capacity as "Leader of the Last Times", he alone could guarantee to his followers an escape from the imminent catastrophe which was going to overwhelm all the Evil Ones.

From these two episodes taken together comes the notion, later on propounded in Proverbs 10:25, that "the *Zaddik* is the Foundation of the World"—put in terms of our two episodes: so long as there are Zaddikim (the Lot story supplies the minimum number, though later Jewish Aggadah was fond of augmenting it), *Heaven and Earth would not pass away* (italics mine).

For perhaps the quintessential statement of what has emerged in this short discussion, it is instructive to turn to the *Zohar*'s explanation of the phrase, "Noah walked with God." Noah was a Righteous Man *(Zaddik)*. Assuredly so after the Supernal (Heavenly) pattern. It is written, "the Righteous One is the foundation of the world", and the Earth is established thereon, for this is the Pillar that upholds the world. So Noah was called *Zaddik* (Righteous) below. All this is implied in the words "Noah walked with God", meaning that he never separated himself from Him and acted so as to be a true copy of the Supernal (or Heavenly) ideal, "a Zaddik the Foundation of the *World*", an embodiment of the world's Covenant of Peace.

Incidentally, this discussion gives us the basis on which to understand the curious statement in the Gospel of Thomas telling the disciples after Jesus' death to go to Jerusalem to James the *Zaddik, "or whose sake Heaven and Earth came into existence"* (italics again mine). It also will allow us to comprehend how the Early Church fathers could have thought that James wore the ephod of the High Priest and entered the Holy of Holies, though a discussion of this is beyond the scope of this monograph.

Here, too, it does not take a very great leap of the imagination—when combining this notion of the essentiality of *"the Zaddik"* with idea of his Priestly prerogatives—to arrive at a synthesis of what constitutes an efficacious atonement for the purposes of avoiding sins of omission and seeking remission for communal sin, i.e., only the atonement made by a proper Priest/*Zaddik* could constitute an efficacious soteriological act. Again to discuss the presentation of Jesus as *Zaddik* in the New Testament, not to mention his Priestly qualifications after the telltale "Order of Melchizedek" in Hebrews or the *"yazdik Zaddik"*—ideology of Isaiah 53:10–11, developed with such telling—if in Palestinian terms illegitimate—effect in Paul's "Justification" theology, is beyond the scope of this monograph.

True, in Palestinian literature of the period, this idea of the necessity of a Priestly *Zaddik* for an efficacious intervention for redemption from sin is nowhere adumbrated in the straightforward theological manner of Paul (although James 5:17's "the fervent working prayer of the Righteous One much effects" implies it), influenced as he was by Greek methods of philosophical argumentation and polemics; still, there is so much jockeying around the notion in Second Temple sectarian literature that it is hard to imagine that some "Opposition" group did not give expression to it in oral form and even perhaps written. Certainly, one finds it in the demands of "the Zealots"—to use Josephus' familiar terminology—in 4 BCE. and later for a Priesthood of Higher Purity and in much of the Qumran speculation centering around "the Sons of Zadok."

In addition to sowing the seeds of the notions of Resurrection of the Dead and apocalyptic—both important aspects of Zaddik-theorizing—Ezekiel provides the essential definition of "the Zaddik" in Chapter 18. He does so almost in an antinomian fashion, over and against the Law in its most literal exposition as found in previous Scripture, that is, he states the later "Ebionite" or "Jewish Christian" doctrine that certain passages in Scripture were not necessarily true and, in particular, expressly countermands the one which would be the most damaging to the ideology of *"the Zaddik"*—the Deuteronomic idea that a man's sins are visited upon his sons.

The man who respects My observances and keeps My laws will not die for his father's sins. Such a son shall certainly live . . . The man who has sinned is the one who must die. A son is not to suffer for the sins of his father, nor a father for the sins of his son.

He also states what essentially becomes the program for much later Christianity, not to mention that found at Qumran:

The *Zaddik* is Law-abiding. We does not. . . seduce his neighbor's wife or sleep with a woman during her periods. He oppresses no one, returns pledges, never steals, gives his own bread to the hungry, his clothes to the naked. He never charges usury on loans, etc.

Finally, laying the basis for what can be seen as the program of John the Baptist (a man also referred to as a "*Zaddik*" in both Josephus and the New Testament) and/or Qumran to follow; he states,

But if the Wicked man renounces all the sins he has committed, respects My laws and is Law-abiding and honest, he will certainly live and not die. All the sins he has committed will be forgotten from then on. He will surely live because of his practice of Righteousness. House of Israel, in the future I mean to judge each of you *by what he does*. . . (italics mine—the "doing" ideology again) Repent. Renounce all your sins, avoid all occasions of sin, shake off all the sins you have committed against Me and make yourselves a new heart and a new spirit. . . Repent and live!

It is, according to this view, sin which brings death and the repentance from sin, life. One sees here just how essential both the abrogation of the Deuteronomic notion of unjustified suffering and the new doctrine of Resurrection of the Dead are in this new scheme of Ezekiel of "the *Ish-Zaddik*" or "the Righteous Man." Formerly, if the Righteous Man suffered, it could be because his ancestors or children had sinned. After Ezekiel's break with this ideology, the idea of another-worldly recompense or individual resurrection became an inevitable development.

The last section of the Prophet Ezekiel must be understood as the "Zadokite" statement par excellence. It is difficult to think that Ezekiel, or whoever authored this section, was unaware of the possibilities inherent in the play on words between "Zadok" and "Zaddik, " especially in view of his previous use of the term "Zaddik" above. Certainly the exegetes at Qumran understood it in this way and were far less slow than many modern commentators to grasp this central connection, but then perhaps they had direct oral tradition from Ezekiel's time to aid them. At Qumran the terminology "Son of Zadok" is interchanged with "Son of *Zedek*" and extended and elaborated further into the conception of "the *Moreh-Zedek*"/"The Teacher of Righteousness."

In exegesis at Qumran, the key phraseology always played upon in a given text when an interpretation is being related to "the *Moreh-Zedek*", is always "the *Zaddik*"—so much so that the sectaries seem to have done extremely well in picking up almost every passage in Isaiah and Psalms where the word "*Zaddik*" appears. In addition to possibly assuming Ezekiel was setting out the way for the return of Jesus ben Yehozedek -the High Priest of the Return and son of the High Priest before the destruction by Nebuchadnezzar—to power, he would not have been unaware of similar plays inherent in the names of two previous High Priests, associated with Jerusalem, one in Abraham's time and the other in David's, i.e., "Melchizedek" and "Zadok." As "Zadok" was the first High Priest to officiate in Solomon's Temple, Jesus ben Yehozedek was the first High Priest to officiate in the reconstructed Second Temple after the return from Babylon.

Though all of this word play might simply be coincidental, whether this Jesus was an actual or spiritual descendent of Solomon's Zadok is something which must remain questionable despite the official genealogies provided. The Qumran exegetes were as aware of the possibilities inherent in the terminology, "Melchizedek", as the Christians who followed them. Despite difficulties in reconstruction, it cannot be denied that 11Q Melchizedek is using the phraseology "Men of the Lot of Melchizedek" in the same manner that the Damascus Document is using the term "Sons of Zadok" and, therefore by reduction, "Zadok" and "Melchizedek" correspond in some way.

When Ezekiel uses the phrase "Sons of Zadok" (40:46, 43:19, 44:15, and 48:11), he uses it in contradistinction to another previous group who, if those who contend a direct genealogical link back to the "Zadok" of Solomon's Temple are correct, must be seen as the ongoing "Zadokite Hierarchy." These "have broken My Covenant with their filthy practices." They have admitted foreigners, "uncircumcised in heart and body, to frequent My Sanctuary and profane My Temple." Here is a clear echo of the Phineas/Ezra mentality, so important for understanding the later 'Zealot' sectarianism of the Second Temple Period ('sectarian' only after the coming of the Romans and the Pharisaic/Herodian takeover). It is reinforced with: "No foreigner, uncircumcised in mind and body, is to enter My Sanctuary." Ezekiel alludes to the previous Governing Priestly Establishment with the words, "They have deputized someone else to perform their duties in the Sanctuary."

In his midnight journey, taken with the aid of the Holy Spirit—a journey suspiciously similar to Muhammad's *mir'aj* and *isra'*—he had already seen "the sons of Shaphan (a family prominent in finding 'the Book of the Law' and the 'Reform' of Josiah) and others observing all manner of filthy practices." If this Establishment was "Zadokite" before Ezekiel's time (though there is no convincing proof of this), then "the Zadokites" of Ezekiel's usage must differ in some way from them. If it was not, then the terminology is new. Either way, as Ezekiel uses it, it comprises a qualitative element, notably "the Levites, the Priests, the Sons of Zadok" are "those who did their duty in the Sanctuary when the Israelites strayed from Me."

The Establishment, including "the sons of Shaphan", are those "Levites who abandoned Me when Israel strayed far from Me to follow idols." This is precisely the passage which is going to be seized upon below in Column IV of the Damascus Document below to make its all-important definition—and this is going to turn out to be an esoteric one—of who these new "*Bnei-Zadok Levitical Priests*" are. The previous ones are to be punished—in Ezekiel's words—by menial service in the Temple where "*They are to hold themselves at the service of the People*" *as they used to se are never to approach Me again to perform the Priestly Office in My Presence*. . .(italics mine)."

What is being countenanced here is nothing less than a change in the Priesthood. The new Priestly Establishment is to be "*ha-Leva'im ha-Cohanim Bnei-Zadok*" or, to paraphrase in English, "the Levites who are Bnei-Zadok Priests." At this point, if we insert the esoteric exegesis we are suggesting, the result is "those Levites who are Righteous Priests" or, if one prefers "Sons of Righteousness" Priests, which accords with Ezekiel's own words, i.e. those Levites "who did their duty to Me in the Sanctuary" or those among the "Sons of Zadok who did not go astray from Me."

An interesting follow-up to what is occurring here is that, when John Hyrcanus assumed the High Priesthood (c. 130 BCE), he did so subject to the coming of another "Prophet" who would make a final determination of the situation. Here we have in Josephus' words something of the "True Prophet" ideology which was to so bedevil the Second Temple Period and beyond—particularly where both Qumran and the succeeding group of "Jamesian Christians", called by Early Church fathers "*Ebionites*", were concerned—which shows that it was Prophets who determined who was to serve at God's altar, not genealogy, conflicting assertions notwithstanding. The sequence laid down by Ezekiel was theoretically to stand until a final determination was to be made by a coming "Prophet"—thereafter, widely known as the "True Prophet", in contradistinction to all the other "Lying" ones—would be inaugurated. It is the view of this paper that this is "the Zadokite Priesthood" we are delineating here.

We do not claim to be the first to see the basis of "the Zadokite Priesthood" in the notion of "the Zaddik." "The

Priesthood after the Order of Melchizedek" is just a variation of it and Epiphanius in the Fifth Century understood the two conceptions to be related—assuming that what he meant by "Sadducee" was equivalent to what we are calling "Zadokite" here. Nor does the transliteration "Sadducee" fit the spelling of the name "Zadok" in the Septuagint. If we ignore for the moment the description of the Sadducee Party as we have it in Josephus and the New Testament and see the conception—whatever else it may be—as equivalent to what was meant in the Dead Sea Scrolls by "Sons of Zadok", then the discrepancies in spelling pass away and *"Zaddouki"* becomes reduceable to *"Zuddiki"* just as easily as it does to *"Zadoki."*

Characteristics like "being more strict in Judgment", as signaled in the Pseudoclementine Recognitions, have a telling effect here too. The Karaites in the Middle Ages, who were also styled by themselves and others "Sadducees", just as often referred to themselves as *"Zaddikim"* as well. In this regard, the Karaite writer al-Kirkisani does see Jesus as coming after "Zadok" and having the same doctrine as him. Notices of this kind have received only the most cursory examination from scholars. J. Le Moyne's well-known book on *The Sadducees (Les Saduceans)* considers a linguistic derivation, such as this, from *"Zaddik"* impossible but adduces no reasons why, except to say in an aside that one can see no reason why the Sadducees in their origins or appearance should qualify as being "Just", meaning "Righteous." Of course not, if one were only going to consider Establishment Sadducees or Herodian ones like those pictured in Josephus and the New Testament. But if one were going to take into consideration those at Qumran, well that is obviously another story—of course Le Moyne, conventional scholar that he was, does not consider "the Sadducees" at Qumran at all. Even the famous American doyen of archeology, W. F. Albright, earlier in the Century, felt it was necessary to go deeper into this kind of consideration and promised an article in the future, which he never wrote.

Three writers, however, did to a greater or lesser extent; but their work has been almost totally ignored in the somewhat superficial speculation that surrounds the origins of the "Sadducee" or "Zadokite Movement." These were J. Bowman, R. North, and P. Wemberg-Moller. The latter even spelled out with unmistakable precision the dependence of *"Zadok"* upon *"Zaddik"* and, in an article in the 1950's: "Ezekiel and the Zadokite Priesthood", showed fairly convincingly that the Aaronid Priesthood originated in the time of Ezra or later, being a designation used to denote conflicting groups of Priests, Zadokites and—what he called—Abiatharites. He then emphasized the cruciality of the "Zealot-related claim of "the zeal of Phineas" for establishing all "Zadokite" High-Priestly claims—Phineas being a patronym of "Zadok." According to this view, the "Zadokite" claims in Ezekiel ("the Zadokite Covenant") and the "Zealot"/"Zeal of Phineas" claims ("the Zealot Covenant") made in both the Maccabee Books and Hebrew Ben Sira on the basis of Numbers 25, would be identical.

Though a full discussion of these matters is beyond the scope of this monograph, some areas perhaps need further precisification. In Nehemiah, it is specifically claimed that some of the returning clans making up the twenty-four Priestly courses mentioned in Chronicles cannot prove their genealogies—some are even said not to be priestly at all! If this is true, it attests to the artificiality of almost all claims and surviving genealogical records from this period. Herod probably completed the chaos by destroying whatever was left of these records and, in the process, brought in the new *"Sadduceean* Priesthood," which we call for the purposes of discussion, following the *Talmud* and Karaite sources (one must call them something), "Boethusians", not "Zadokites." The New Testament often has them as "Herodians."

Even much more striking in this regard, the Book of Ezra gives Ezra the same genealogy as Jesus ben Yehozedek, a patent impossibility, which in itself is revealing, for it shows something of the scramble in this period to get the right genealogy. It is of the same genre of reliability as the two conflicting genealogies the Gospels of Matthew and Luke provide for Jesus, each of which give a different father for the same character Shaltiel (also from this period). In Ezra's case, it is also clear that the Phineas-related "Zealot" claim—which Bowman identifies with "the Zadokite Covenant"—is being employed (perhaps even for one of the first times after the fall of the Temple), since in his/Ezra's "zeal for the Law", he causes backsliders, including those from the High-Priestly family itself, one of whom he exiles North—possibly the inception of the Samaritan "Zadokite" line—to put away their non-Judean wives or be excommunicated (Phineas would have slain them, but Ezra had probably not the authority to go this far).

Mattathias the Hasmonaean and father of Judas Maccabee, of course, is depicted in 1 Macc. 2:24–28 as doing just this—and on the altar at Modein no less, whatever altar this might have been at this time. It also shows there was some question as to exactly what comprised a High Priest in Ezra's time (c. 450 BCE) and, at least metaphorically if not genealogically, Ezra is being depicted as something like one—this despite the fact that Jesus Ben Yehozedek's (again note the "Zadokite" implications of the latter's patronym), shall we say, previously "Zadokite" family had seemingly been entrenched in Jerusalem earlier. For Ezra's part, he presides at ceremonies and, all-in-all, replicates many of Nehemiah's actions in the Book by his name, resembling nothing so much as "a *Nusi*" or "Community Leader." Yet the fact that he is supplied with a proper High-Priestly genealogy (no matter that it is the same as Jesus Ben Yehozedek's—Jesus' too, is hardly very convincing when one takes into consideration generation counts) shows there were some who saw Ezra as a kind of High Priest as well; and certainly he had power over the High Priest whichever descendant of Jesus ben Yehozedek it may have been at this time.

The missing link between the two conceptions of the High Priesthood—"the Zealot" and "the Zadokite"—is to be found in the Hebrew version of Ecclesiasticus (also known, as noted above, as "Ben *Sira* ", after its author's colophon) in a portion which has—for obvious reasons—not been preserved in the Greek. This work very pointedly develops towards extolling the High Priestly qualifications of Simeon the *Zaddik,* a key figure for the Second Century BCE and thereafter, as all lines of tradition seem to go back to him as they do earlier to Ezra.

In the all-important final section that goes in the English by the phrase, "In Praise of Famous Men" (now that we know the Hebrew, we know it is rather "Anshei-Hesed"/"Men of Piety," an important distinction as "Piety" is one of the key concepts of the period to follow), beginning with Noah the *Zaddik* (also an important cognomen for what is to follow) and ending with Simeon; this document, often thought of as being "Sadduceean", provides a list of such *"Hassidim"* (echoed in similar rehearsals in Wisdom, Jubilees, and the Qumran Damascus Document), who must therefore be thought of as *"Zaddikim"* as well (the terminology is used interchangeably at Qumran as it is in Isaiah, Enoch, and here). Because in this section of Ecclesiasticus, "Zadokite" and "Zealot" claims are linked and centered around identifiable *"Zaddikim"* or *"Hassidim"*—in particularly this *"Simeon the Zaddik"* who also forms a fulcrum of Talmudic tradition (apparently Ben *Sira's* grandfather); this book constitutes a kind of passport to Priestly claims in the Second Temple Period and is to be found in most all centers of sectarian activity i.e., "Zealot", "Essene", "Karaite", and "Christian", all of which are non-Pharisaic, which is probably the reason for its exclusion from the Old Testament canon transmitted by Rabbinic tradition.

Onias the Just or Onias the *Zaddik* is the last "Righteous" High Priest before the Hasmonaean succession. As far as 2 Macc. is concerned, anyhow, and demonstrably Daniel and Enoch (including those portions found at Qumran), the succession cannot and does not follow the blood line—whatever modem scholars might latterly have us believe—since Onias' brother Jason is implicitly excluded from it because of his "Godlessness" and "lmpiety" (2 Macc. 4:13). In just the opposite manner, "Onias the *Zaddik*" is a man, through whose "Piety" *(Hesed)* the Law was observed *"us perfectly us possible"* (italics mine—*n.b.,* the Qumran and New Testament overtones again in the allusion to "Perfection"). At this point, not only do we have a 'Zadokite' claim, in the sense we have expounded it, being laid over whatever genealogical one he might have had previously; but what we should also term a "Hassidaean" and a "Zealot" one, since the text also calls him "zealous for the Law," just as Ben Sira does in his picture of Onias' father Simeon (also a "Righteous One")—though all these terminologies, as the reader by now might suspect, are simply variations on a similar theme.

At Qumran, besides the employment of all these vocabularies with the same intended effect, "Ebionite" imagery (i.e., "the Poor")—a designation for both the Communities of James the Just and one of self-designation at Qumran—is also introduced. It is equally noteworthy that another parallel term is used to describe this Onias in 2 Macc., that is "Oz" or "*Ma'oz le-'Amo*", as Eusebius via Hegesippus uses to describe James the Zaddik (a.k.a. and widely referred to as "the brother of Jesus,"), i.e. "Protector of his Fellow Countrymen': or, in James' case, "Protection of the People." A similar terminology can be detected in the Qumran Damascus Document (see *MZCQ*).

In the sometimes superficial way a good deal of Dead Sea Scroll research has progressed, the Maccabees are usually taken to be a Priest line that "usurped" the High Priestly role from a previous reigning or more legitimate one; but this is quite clearly at odds with almost all the available evidence and is only propounded to aid a theory of identification that would cast one or the other of the Maccabeans as illegitimate and appropriate candidates for the "Wicked Priest" of Qumran literature. In the Book of Daniel, which must be considered a contemporary report on these events, there is no interruption seen between the death of Onias and the rising of those called "the Kedoshim" there ("Saints"), i.e., Judas' Army. In the Book of Enoch, no interruption is signaled between the death of the Simeon/Onias "the Righteous" line and the rise of Judas and this in passages extant at Qumran.

In 1 Macc. 2:24–6, much is made of the Phineas-style "zeal" of Judas' father Mattathias, i.e., a "Zealot"-style High Priestly claim (which Bowman would identify with "the Zadokite Covenant")—in addition to the genealogical one—is being made on behalf of the whole family. In any event, the family is pointedly identified in the same passages as being of the first and principal Priestly clan of Jehoiarib. There can be little doubt that this is a "Zadokite" clan, so this is a "Zadokite" Priestly where was the "usurpation"? Such ideas of "usurpation" only exist in their detractors' heads and are only put forth to demonize them as candidates for the now-famous Qumran pejorative, "the Wicked Priest"—definitely an Establishment High Priest whom those writing these documents opposed. In any event, perhaps it was to claim such indisputable "Zadokite" descent that the Maccabeans claimed attachment to this first and most important Priestly course, since there nowhere exists any delineation of which clans are Zadokite and which Abiatharid (i.e., Eleazarid and Ithamarid—parallel lines descended in theory from Aaron's two children).

As far as Judas is concerned, it is always ignored by commentators—when they identify Judas' brother Jonathan as the first Maccabean to hold the High Priesthood—that in both 1 Macc. and Josephus, Judas was "elected" to the High

Priesthood three times, a typical "Zealot" procedure in this Period which gathers in strength during the First Century CE and is alluded to as well quite overtly in the Community Rule at Qumran.

It is perhaps more accurate to say that Jonathan Maccabean to accept bestowal of the High Priesthood upon him *from foreign hands*, a thing abjured by Mattathias Judas' nephew by his brother Simon, John Hyrcanus of his son Alexander Jannaeus and the latte Aristobulus), and probably the sine qua non of a p High Priestly Line, that is, except so far as later ' "Herodian Sadducees" (who were certainly not the same as Qumran "Sadducees") were concerned. In any event, there can be little doubt that Judas presided over the cleansing of the Temple in the manner of a powerful Vicegerent like Ezra or a High Priest (moreover, this is obviously an action inspiring the similar episode relating to Jesus in the New Testament, particularly in the Gospel of John, where the same "Zealot" claim is raised for Jesus, i.e., *"Zeal for Your House consumes me"* —2:13–17).

But Judas is clearly also a *Zaddik*. 2 Macc 5:27 identifies him in no uncertain terms as such, averring that he and nine others (i.e., the proverbial *"Ten Zaddikim"* of the Lot story above) went into the wilderness and lived on berries and roots "to avoid contracting defilement." It should also be immediately clear to anyone who has sensitive historical antennae that this is a progenitor of the John the Baptist story approximately two centuries earlier. It should also be clear to those sensitive to "*Zaddik*'ite symbolism (now, if we can make this jump, also "Zadokite" symbolism of an esoteric kind) that all of what we were earlier expounding concerning Proverbs' and, for that matter, the *Zohar* of mystical *Kabbalah* Tradition's "*the Zaddik the Foundation of the World*" is being suggested if not embodied in an episode such as this. By implication, it also gives a pointed reminder that Judas. is a direct successor to "*Onias the Zaddik*" or "the Just"—and, for that matter, his father, the hero of *Ben Sira* (found at both Qumran and Masada but not in Rabbinic literature), if *any* such reminder were by now necessary.

Schematically, Chapter Three of 2 Macc. opens in praise of Onias' "*Piety*", his saintly acts, and his role as "*Zaddik*" or "*Protection*" or "*Shield of the People.*" It closes in 15:11–24 with Onias together with Jeremiah—personifying "the Ancient of Days"—handing the "Messianic" Sword of the Battle Priest/ Zaddik (the "*Messiah Zidkeinu*" of common Jewish prayer and a precursor of sorts to the English "King Arthur" legends) to Judas. There is no interruption signaled and, indeed, there was none despite the flight of another descendent, Onias IV, to Egypt. The same "Zadokite" and "Zealot" High Priestly claims are being put forth for Simeon the *Zaddik*, Onias the *Zaddik*, Judas' father Mattathias, and Judas as, indeed, they are later to the discerning eye for Jesus and his brother James in New Testament and Early Church Literature. The notion of a genealogical succession we owe to an imperfect understanding of Chronicles fostered by Josephus who, indeed too, had much to lose and be embarrassed about if the truth were out. On the other hand, Josephus may have been so ignorant or simply considered so untrustworthy that the esoteric understanding of these matters escaped him or was never communicated to him —something the writer finds difficult to credit.

One or two historical notes are crucial here. What party the Maccabees belonged to has been debated. According to this view, there can be little doubt that originally they were Sadducees. The discrepancy between 1 Macc. 7:14–5 and 2 Macc 14:6–14 concerning whether Judas was leader of the Hassidaeans, "everyone a stout fighting man, a volunteer on the side of the Law", is also relatively easily resolved following this view. The Hassidaeans were the Party of Judas, the Party of Apocalyptic, par excellence and, as most commentators have grasped, probably responsible for literature like Daniel, Enoch, and the like. As such, they are also "Zadokite" (in the sense of "*Zaddikite*") and, therefore, certainly related to the foundations of both "the Zealot Movement" and "the Messianic" one and, what some might call "Christianity in Palestine"—but one must use this terminology with care as even Acts avers that "Christians were first called Christians in Antioch" in Syria, not Palestine ("*Essenes*" would probably do very much better, but here too one must use it with care and has to know what one means by it). Judas is undeniably their teacher and leader.

This group, as I have been suggesting, is linked to the sectaries at Qumran, as even most commentators have realized in their rather simplistic adherence to "Essene"— theorizing; but, once again, one has to know which "Essenes" or "Hassidaeans" these were and at what period; because there is also a group of break- away "Hassidaeans"—the ones depicted 1 Macc. 7 above—and which I have delineated very extensively in *MZCQ*. Therefore, those who would see "the Pharisees" also as being descended from "the Hassidaeans" are correct too, because both "the Pharisees" and the sectaries at Qumran (and presumably Josephus' "Zealots" or "Fourth Philosophy" and "the Messianic Movement" as well) believe in "the Resurrection of the Dead" as did, according to 2 Macc., Judas' Movement too.

But the terminology "Pharisee" has not been employed because it is just developing. 1 Macc., which rather emanates from the world of Judas' less-xenophobic nephew, John Hyrcanus, is not really being written from a pro-Judas point-of-view, but rather something more intermediate or what some have called a pro-family point-of-view, extending Mattathias' "Zealot Covenant" to the whole family, whether deservedly or not. The distinction is quite clear—what I am called "break-away Hassidaeans" or "Pharisees" (as explained in *MZCQ*, what we are witnessing here is really the birth moment of "the Pharisee Party"—not "the Hassidaean") are willing to accept the appointment of a High Priest from foreign hands—in this case the Seleucid Syrians. Later it will be the Romans and Herodians, which is why Qumran so disapproves of such "Phariseeizers" and calls them "*Seekers after Smooth Things*." Accordingly, Jonathan and Simon, Judas' brothers, must be seen as proto-Pharisees, followed by John Hyrcanus, his grandson Hyrcanus II (but not the latter's brother Aristobulus I1 who opposes both the Roman and Herodian take-over of Palestine) and the Herodian and Procuratorial High Priests.

For their part, what we call in *MZCQ* "the Purist Hassidaeans" or "Zadokites" repudiate any such a procedure, as do the later so-called "Essenes", "Zealots" and, shall we say, "Messianists" succeeding to them. They view only a national or native Priesthood as authentic and often their method—as "the Zealots" and those at Qumran later and Judas earlier -is "election." Along these lines, one must group Judas, Alexander Jannaeus, Honi (*n.b.*, in Josephus, this 'resistance' "Prophet" denounces the Romans, the Pharisees who support their entrance into the country, and their Herodian enablerss, espousing the nationalist/"Zealot" line of Alexander's son Aristobulus II, and pays with his life because of it), Aristobulus himself, who also ends up paying with his life as does his son, John the Baptist, Judas the Galilean, his two sons James and Simon, Josephus' "*Sadduk*", Jesus, James, "the Prophet" Josephus calls "Ananias," etc.

"The Sadducees", who appear after the Romans and Herod take power, are not the same as "the Sadducees" who existed before them and, therefore, I would rather call the former group "Purist Sadducees"—or even, if one prefers "Messianic Sadducees", which some might see as a contradiction in terms, but which Qumran most certainly exemplifies—while the latter, who are a kind of Phariseeizing "Sadducee" group, best referred to as "Herodian Sadducees" or "Boethusians" (after the High Priest Herod imported from Egypt), accept appointment of High Priests by foreigners (this is the crucial determining factor), accept foreign occupation (some even prefer it), follow "the Traditions of the Elders" (i.e., "the Oral Law"), accept niece marriage, etc. By the time of John the Baptist, we are no longer talking about a Party in the official orbit, as its activities are by this time circumscribed and illegal (i.e., from the time of Judas and Zadok or the "Sadduk a Pharisee" of Josephus onwards).

From this point, we are correct in talking about "an Opposition Priesthood" or "High Priesthood", i.e. one centering around "the *Zaddik*", "*Priest-Zaddik*", or "*Moreh-Zedek*"/"Teacher of Righteousness" as at Qumran or any given generation—a kind of "*Hidden Imam*" to use Islamic terminology (which, indeed, seems directly related to it) or, for a modern parallel, a kind of Khomeini-like Movement, though with a somewhat different ideology. This is "the Movement"—and it is "*a Movement*"— that gives rise to the literature at Qumran. It is an underground Movement of vast proportions that later moves into *Kabbalah*, "*Jewish Christianity*" or "*Ebionitism*" (a better terminology), Islam, Shi'ism, and Jewish *Karaism*, not to mention an assortment of other groups and sects. The central notion of the whole is "the Zaddik-idea and the Zadokite Priesthood", which later morphs into other variations like "a Priesthood after the Order of Melchizedek and the Islamic "*Imamate*."

Let us now finally look at the Qumran documents and see how all these claims are put together. In Column IV of the Damascus Document where Ezekiel 44:15's "Zadokite Covenant" is expounded, already noted above, the reference is to:

> The Holy Men of Former Times (who must be seen as identical to "the Anshei-Hesed" or "Men of Piety" with which Ecclesiasticus/*Ben Sira begins*) whose sins God forgave and who justified the Righteous (*yazdiku-Zaddik*) and condemned the wicked

(yarshi'u-Resha'im—notions running close to Paul's theology centering about Jesus and based on the terminology of Isaiah 53:11)

These are designated as equivalent to or, really, as the definition of "the Sons of Zadok" of Ezekiel 44: 15. Associated with both of these is a conception of predestined pre-existence, as we have it in regard to "the *Zaddik*" in the *Zohar* and the Gospel of Thomas (translated in the Gospel of John and transformed with regard to Jesus into the *Logos*-doctrine). Not only has God "foreknow" the "ways of the Wicked" from before

> the beginning of the world. . ., their end has always been predetermined. . . Nevertheless in all of their generations He has ever raised up for Himself men called by Name, so that He might provide survival for the earth and fill the face of the world with their seed.

Here allusion is being made, not only to the first *Zaddik* Noah, but to the role and function of the "*Zaddikim*" in the world. In the next sentence "the *Zaddik*-idea" is linked to "the Messianic" with the words:

> And to these has He ever revealed his Holy Spirit at the hands of His Messiah. . ., and He has clearly specified who they were.

Finally in the words in this passage identifying "the Sons of Zadok" with "the Elect of Israel who would stand in the Last Days", it is stated that

> their names have been specified, the families into which they are to be born, the Epochs in which they are to function. . .,

> a clear presentation of the notion of "the pre-existent Zaddik."

This is further echoed and strengthened in the Qumran

Hymns by the words "You established their destiny before ever they were", i.e.,

> Before ever my father begat me, You knew me. From the womb of my mother, You showered me with Holiness. . .For my father knew me not and my mother abandoned me to You. You are a Father to all the Sons of Your Truth.

And finally:

> You alone created the Zaddik and established him from the womb. . .You have marked the Spirit of the Zaddik (*Ruah ha-Zaddik*). . . and no man can be justified except through You (again, the "Justification" ideology). Therefore I implore You by the Spirit which You gave (me) to Perfect Your pieties (Hesedeicha—here is the "Perfection" ideology again, also found in the Damascus Document and Community Rule at Quman) to your Servant (and "the Servant" ideology), purifying me by your Holy Spirit (Ruah Kedosheicha—to say nothing of "the Holy Spirit" one, also alluded to above in the Damascus Document and generously referred to in the Community Rule as well).

These statements in the Qumran Hymns, not only identify "the *Zaddik*-idea" with that of the "Sonship" one and this, as just signaled, against a background of "Justification" theology; but they provide us with an idea of how the Early Church fathers, Eusebius in the Fourth Century and Epiphanius in the Fifth (both probably basing themselves on Hegesippus in the Second), could have considered one such "*Zaddik*"/"*Moreh-Zedek*" James, "*a Nazirite from his mother's womb*" (italics mine).

In the Damascus Document, the esoteric aspects of Ezekiel's "Zadokite Covenant" are heightened and extended to such a degree that others who would consider themselves "Zadokite" by some more genealogical yardstick—for instance, the accommodating and compromising "Priesthood"'s functioning under both Herod and the Roman Procurators—could hardly be considered "Sadduceean" at all, at least in the sense of being "Zadokite." In this manner, the Law-oriented, xenophobic "Righteousness" of an Ezra, Phineas, Ezekiel, or Mattathias is pushed to its final extreme.

Moreover, in their rendering of Ezekiel 44:15, the difficulties inherent in the original phraseology: "*Ha-Leva'im ha- Cohanim Bnei-Zadok*" are eliminated as the sectaries take the liberty of adding, in the interests of their own exegesis, waw-constructs ("and" s) between the nouns, splitting the appositives and breaking the genitive constructs, so that the singular nominative is separated out into the three distinct categories they desire to expound. Often great liberties are taken with textual material in this way at Qumran in the interests of a certain exegesis as they are, for instance, in the New Testament, thereby increasing the resemblance between the two *modii operandii*; and, in this case, it is fairly certain that the passage in question is not being reproduced with precision but, rather, to enhance a desired exposition and make it absolutely clear, as various other parts, unimportant to the general thrust of the passage, are also sometimes omitted in both environments.

"Priests" are defined as "the Penitents of Israel who went out from the Land of Judah" (phraseology reprised later in the Document where it is said they went "into the Land of Damascus", from which our modern nomenclature for the Document is taken), hardly a normative definition of "Priests" in the usual sense of the word as we saw. Even more noteworthy, the expression "Levites" is transformed into the usage "*Nilvim*"/ "Joiners", i.e., as the Damascus Document expresses it, "the Joiners with them"; and this is obviously done purposefully, since "*Nilvim*" is a term known from both Isaiah and Esther where it signifies "Converts" or "Gentiles", i.e., those attaching

themselves to the Jewish Community in some manner—
something like the way the terminology "God-Fearers" is used
in the New Testament and Early Church literature; and, in
fact, this terminology ("God-Fearers') and/or variations of it
("fearing God") is widely present in succeeding Columns of the
Damascus Document, particularly at its end. This could mean
that there was a cadre of Gentile "God-Fearers" attached to
the Community or .'Movement" and not only do I think, but
a Movement like Paul's "Gentile Mission" certainly suggests,
there was.

As just indicated (but it bears repeating):

> The Sons of Zadok are the Elect of Israel who will
> stand in the Last Days. . . the Men of Holiness
> (or "Saints"), through whom (or "by whom") God
> would make atonement. . . and they will justify
> the Righteous and condemn the Wicked (i.e., pure
> "Justification" theology as already noted).

According to this presentation, "Priests" are not Priests
at all. On the contrary, it is specifically noted that they are
ordinary Israelites, i.e., they are not "Zadokites" as "the Sons
of Zadok" are—they are not even Aaronic. They may be, but
they may not be. This is not their distinguishing characteristic.
Their distinguishing characteristic is that they are "Penitents
in the desert"—terminology, as noted, repeated later in the
Document and reminiscent of John the Baptist's activities.

As with the original. Ezekiel, the thrust here is qualitative
again, not necessarily genealogical. "The Sons of Zadok", in the
language and exposition of the Damascus Document, are quite
clearly the quintessence of their generation and the high point
of the whole ideology. They are the "Saints" as it were or, if
one prefers, "the Holy Men"—a direct appositive ("*Kedoshim*"
in Daniel)—and the Zaddikim "who will stand," "wait," or
perhaps even "be resurrected" (to use the "standing" language

in the manner of "the bones" passage in Ezekiel, as we can see, perhaps the most favorite prophet at Qumran) in the Last Days" or "at the End of Time" to "Justify the Righteous and condemn the Wicked." That is, seemingly, they are to take part in—just as in 'Christian' ideology—what is normally called, "the Last Judgment." Elsewhere at Qumran, they are also referred to as "the Sons of *Zedek*", i.e., "The Sons of Righteousness" (an expression known to the Gospels as well) or, as the Qumran Hymns would put it, "the Sons of Your Truth"—all this against a very carefully-adumbrated background of "the Righteousness of works", i.e., the "*ma'aseichem*", so often referred to in this Document, Hymns, and throughout the Qumran corpus and echoed, not surprisingly, in the Letter of James (to say nothing of in the Koran).

To sum up: the beginning of the Qumran orientation is to be found in a succession of *Zaddiks*, starting with Simeon the Zaddik and coming down through his son or descendant, the martyred Onias, and Judas surnamed the Maccabee (a title also alluded to in the Qumran Hymns). In some way, persons of this kind are associated with the original "Hassidaean Movement", particularly as depicted by Daniel, probably a pseudonym of the original "Zadokite" one, taken in the sense of those who follow "the *Zaddik*" or are "*Zaddikim*". Both kinds of usages appear liberally at Qumran, not to mention terms like "the Ebionim"/ "The Poor", "Hesed" ("Piety", from which the terminology "Hassidaean" is derived), and "Kedoshim"/"Holy Ones" or "Saints" as, for instance, in Daniel, and various combinations of these like "the Ebionei-Hesed" found in the Qumran Hymns and used as a term of self-designation, i.e., "the Poor Ones of Piety." "The Poor" are even cited several times as the name of "the Community" (i.e., "the Community of the Poor") in the Commentary on Psalm 37.

At Qumran, Ezekiel's ambiguous statements about this new "Priesthood" of "the Sons of Zadok" have been deliberately opened up to include all Israelites and the genealogical thrust, if ever intended, has been discarded. The "Sons of Zadok"-aspect has been extended to produce the meaning of "those who are saved in any and all generations." That we are dealing with a "Supernal" or "Perfection Priesthood" of some kind (scholars like Robert Eisler in the last Century would have it an "Opposition One" with which we are in accord) of "Righteous Ones", as well as an earthly one "standing", "waiting", or "being resurrected to function at the End of Time", is hardly to be questioned.

The step from here to "the Priesthood after the Order of Melchizedek" in Christianity, developing out of it, is not very great—in fact, as already mentioned, there is even a "Melchizedek" Document at Qumran. Whether these Qumran documents pertain to the Second or First Centuries BC, as many scholars have argue, or to the First Century CE, as some of the rest of us do, is not the question. Certainly some of the documents go back to an earlier time, but the question is whether the so-called "sectarian documents" or those never seen before do either in whole or in part. Where this paper is concerned, it is important only in so far as understanding when the notion of a "Son of Zadok" was no longer taken genealogically, but allegorically, and linked to "the Zaddik-idea" as we have been expounding it here. That it was at some point taken completely esoterically or allegorically, having little or no relationship, except metaphorically, to the "Zadok" of David and Solomon's time seems fairly clear.

"RE-ERECTING THE FALLEN TENT OF DAVID" IN A LAND NORTH OF DAMASCUS AND NORTHERN SYRIA

In several papers and the book *James The Brother of Jesus* (Viking/Penguin, 1997–98) we have suggested that the addressee of *"MMT"* is not a king in Palestine at all, but a foreign king and convert to Judaism—therefore his "zeal"; no 'Jewish' kings in Palestine at this time had this kind of "zeal"— namely the King Eusebius calls "the Great King of the Peoples beyond the Euphrates." The allusion is from a document Eusebius claims to have found and personally translated from the Edessene archives. Since Eusebius hardly ranks as a creative writer, we to some extent probably must honor this claim.

In similar venues we have been claiming that Queen Helen of Adiabene and her kinsmen had much to do with the support of the installation we now know as "Qumran." We would like to pursue these theses further by analyzing the Messianic language of the Damascus Document, which claims that "the fallen tent of David" (Amos 9: 11–12) will be rebuilt in a land "North of Damascus" and uses the "Damascus" language generally to express this (Column VII.13–16).

It should be noted that this "fallen tent of David" language from Amos 9:11 is used in the speech attributed to James just before he sends his representatives "down to Antioch" with his "epistle" containing his "rulings" in Acts 15:13–21 's somewhat tendentious account of what has come to be called "the Jerusalem Council." Our purpose here is to show how many of these references, including an emphasis in the polemics from all sides on the salvationary state of Abraham, can be looked upon in terms of important conversions taking place in Northern Syria at this time (the 30s–40s CE), particularly in Edessa (now "Urfa", but formerly Antioch-by-Callirhoe) as well as further East.

In this context, we will try to show as well that "*MMT*", the first half of which focuses in large measure on the subject of banning "food sacrificed to idols", links up with these parallel bans in Acts and to some extent practised by Josephus' "Essenes"—it should be appreciated from the start that while Paul knows the ban on "things sacrificed to idols", he does not consider it obligatory or even salutatory. Not only this, but T also focuses on Abraham's salvationary state, comparing its "kingly" addressee's "works" to those of Abraham.

Before doing so, however, a few words about AMS carbon dating are in order which, unfortunately, in recent times are necessary because of the amount of misinformation that has been circulated concerning these tests and their so-called 'results'. The first persons to call for AMS carbon dating of Qumran documents were the Prof. Philip Davies and the author of this monograph. This was in a letter to the then Head of the Israel Antiquities Authority Amir Drori on May 5, 1989—the height of the struggle to free the Scrolls and copied to selected persons.

We had written him earlier in March of that year attaching a copy of a similar letter to Prof. John Strugnell, then of Harvard and Head of the International Team", asking for specific access to certain Qumran plates of the unpublished fragments of the Damascus Document. By this time, he did not know it, but we had the official Ministry computerized printout of all Qurnran Documents, published and unpublished, and could specify photographs by name and number exactly what plates we wanted. This probably surprised him too and, because of this, our request came as something of a shock to the responsible parties. However by May we had given up on receiving any positive response to our request for access to specific plates of the Damascus Document fragments.

Therefore we adopted another tack and addressed our complaints to Mr. Drori and enclosed the latest data on AMS carbon dating in case he was not familiar with the process. Our contention was that he could at least exercise his fiat by conducting AMS carbon tests on Qumran documents to test dating claims based on paleographic or handwriting style-sequencing. As a caveat to this, we requested as well that so-called "opposition scholars" like ourselves be included in the process, since they were the ones who clearly felt the most need for such testing and could presumably specify which documents were worth examining.

This too fell on deaf ears and was ignored, but our response actually came several months later when the Israelis themselves announced that they were going to conduct just such AMS carbon tests, but not in association with us, but rather with—of all persons—John Strugnell (now deceased)! Needless to say, they never acknowledged where the initial proposals to conduct such tests came from, but there is an old saying, "imitation is the sincerest form of flattery." Of course "opposition scholars" such as ourselves who had proposed the testing in the first place were completely excluded from the process. This was unfortunate, as the Israel officials in charge and their colleagues, the representatives of the 'official' International Team missed the point, having never felt the need for carbon testing in the first place.

It should be appreciated that we on the other hand never had any illusions about the accuracy of carbon testing where "absolute dating" was concerned. "Absolute dating" is just what it says, attempting an absolute determination of dates. The same can be said for paleography. What we were interested in was what was known as "relative dating", that is, earlier vs. later in the same test run and this primarily to evaluate the accuracy of paleographic sequencing such as it was and of the same "relative" kind. Needless to say, this was never the concern of the Antiquities Authority and their confreres, who did not know what the problems relating to paleographic sequencing even were.

It should be appreciated that the achievement of "absolute dating" is a rarity in radiocarbon dating anyhow. Firstly, in the period of concern to us, there were and are very few real "pegs" as such, as they are called, and much depends upon dendrochronology (tree-ring data analysis and sequencing) and the amount of or lack thereof of impurities that in some manner or other—handling for instance—that may have an Impact on the tests. There was also the known predilection of laboratories to arrive at "results" those requesting the tests to begin with were looking for. This is a rarely understood process, but it is and was there, particularly where all tests concerning the Dead Sea Scrolls were concerned.

Recently in forensics, a science which does not differ appreciably from Radiocarbon analysis, it was found that laboratories, as respected as that of the FBI Crime Lab in Washington D.C., were routinely slanting their reports in exactly this manner and with exactly the same biases. It is doubtful that laboratories as insufficiently credentialed as those involved in the Qumran document tests—most relatively independent of normal academic oversight—would have performed any better being just as apt to fall victim to their own preconceptions and biases. This is particularly evident in the way all the accompanying reports were framed, which were invariably directed against persons like ourselves and quick to cite paleography in support of their conclusions.

The problem is, in the evaluation of radiocarbon evidence, it is little understood by the public at large that a substantial amount of human interpretation is involved, which can appreciably skew final results. That is another reason why "opposition" persons should always be included in the process. Because of the manner in which Qumran materials have been preserved, cleansed, and conserved, there is also a huge amount of impurity which has to be associated with the rendering it otherwise incomprehensible—so no "results" can be achieved at all.

This is why references to "Northern Syria" in the documents under consideration in this writing will be so important and this is why we must be permitted, whatever general preconceptions exist in the academy at large, to consider them and bring them into central focus. The references in question largely occur in the Damascus Document, precisely named because of such references and geographical allusions, but not exclusively so. More to the point, these all circulate about the pivotal citation, familiar to everyone, "the New Covenant in the Land of Damascus", from which the document was given its modern name in the first place—and these, unless taken esoterically, already signal a Syrian milieu of some kind.

Moreover, this is the very document Prof. Davies and the author asked access to, which started the whole modern controversy over the Dead Sea Scrolls in recent years, the field being quite moribund previously—and this, despite the fact that we already had the plates we were asking for in our possession but without "official" permission we were not at liberty to admit we had them. Our point, of course, in making such a request was both to make just this clear and to break the "monopoly" then extant; and this we feel we did in some manner accomplish.

There are also references to a quasi-Syrian milieu in the War Scroll, where "Benjamin" is defined as "the Galut of the Desert", a reference not without significance for Paul's "Benjaminite" pretensions. Here, too, reference is made—probably with future intent—to the return of "the Exiled Sons of Light from the Desert of the Peoples (in our view, the area known as "the Fertile Crescent" or the Syrian Desert) to "the wilderness camp of Jerusalem." "The Peoples" usage (here "*'Amim*" but also "*Go'im*") will be of interest throughout this discussion. "The wilderness" or "desert" in question is clearly distinct from "the Judean" one and probably represents a variation on "the Land of Damascus." The reference is much like the one to "Galilee of the Nations" or "Gentiles" in Matthew 4:15 (here the usual "Ethnon"/"'*Amim*").

Interestingly enough, there are also references in both the New Testament and early Church literature—particularly Eusebius and his above story of the conversion King Agbarus or Abgarus—to Northern Syrian locales. Again, at the time, this would be seen as "the Desert of the Peoples." Moreover, it should be appreciated that the Romans referred to the whole region generally as "Arabia." The same is true in Josephus and his references in *The Jewish War*, Book XX to conversions in the Royal Court of Adiabene, also for our purposes a "Northern Syrian" or, in Roman terms, an "Arabian" locale. The problem is to sort all these parallel or overlapping references out, focus them, and relate them to the same, similar, or parallel events.

Many of the debates in Paul's letters, James, and Hebrews, not only focus on events and arguments in Northern Syrian and neighboring locales, but as well, just as *MMT* does, often turn on Abraham's salvationary state. As noted above, the same is true for Josephus' and, for that matter, the Talmud's picture of the conversion of Queen Helen's sons, Izates and Monobazus, which in particular focuses on the issue of "circumcision" as it was first commanded to Abraham in Genesis 17—an event also alluded to in the Damascus Document.

In the writer's view, this focus on Abraham is neither accidental, incidental, nor coincidental. Even today, citizens of the Turkish city of Urfa, North of Aleppo—formerly the Christian city of .'Edessa" not far from Abraham's origin in Haran—point proudly to "the Pools of Abraham" as a central fixture of their city's topography; and the whole area focuses upon him—this being considered his "Homeland or, at least, the area in which Abraham's father Terah settled after leaving Chaldean Ur in the Book of *Genesis* and from whence Abraham embarked upon his monumental voyage southward to the Land of Canaan. Therefore, Abraham's salvationary state could not have failed to be of interest to the local inhabitants of that area when in search of a paradigmatic soteriological hero.

This is the way Abraham is presented both in Josephus' and the *Talmud's* depiction of Izates' sudden conversion to Judaism under the tutelage of a 'Galilean' teacher by the name of Eleazar (as opposed to an earlier pair, one named "Ananias" and the other probably "Paul" who did not require this—the allusion to "Galilean" here is significant). He is reading, as we saw, Genesis 17 about how Abraham circumcised his entire household and all those traveling with him—implying, as it were, both Gentile and Jew—when asked, just as Acts' "Ethiopian Queen's eunuch", whether he "understood the meaning of the story" he was reading. Whereupon Izates immediately went out and straightaway proceeds to circumcise himself, as does his brother Monobazus. Not only is this a pivotal story, but for the writer, all such paradigmatic citations about Abraham from the literature of this period have in view his use as a exemplary character to be imitated by the inhabitants of this region who identified so much with the story of his origins.

The same is true for the citations of Abraham's faithfulness and his designation as "a Friend of God" (as opposed to an "Enemy"—a term Paul's opponents took pleasure in applying to him) in the Damascus Document—but also for Galatians, Romans, Hebrews, and James, not to mention the Koran. The same is true, as we already saw, for *MMT* which evokes Abraham's salvationary state both at the beginning of the reconstructions as we have it and its end and, again an important pointer for determining its ultimate addressee—but more about this later. It is the position of this article that all documents of this kind were ultimately directed at new converts in a Northern Syrian and/or a related missionary framework where Abraham's origins and his name loomed large.

A final piece in this tangle of parallel sources and allusions is the identification of "Antioch" in many such materials dating back to the First Century with what in other contexts is being called "Edessa." Of course, Edessa is the homeland of Eusebius' "King Agbarus" or "Abgarus" above, whom he also designates as "the Great King of the Peoples beyond the Euphrates" (*n.b.*, how "Peoples" here connects with the War Scroll's "Desert of the Peoples", not to mention Matthew's "Galilee of the Peoples"—a probable parallel allusion). This is an area, certainly contiguous with Queen Helen's and her successor and son King Izates' homeland, Adiabene, which was probably to some extent under "Edessene" control at this time anyhow.

This is, indeed, the sense of the document Eusebius claims to have translated from Edessene 'official' records', reliable or unreliable, not only as "the King of the Edessenes", but also of "the Peoples beyond the Euphrates"—once again, the designation "Peoples" being crucial for the purposes of Paul's own characterization of his "Mission" in this area to these same "*Ethne*"/"Gentiles"/or "Peoples." There is, also, a suggestion in both Syriac and Armenian sources, just as there is in Eusebius, that Queen Helen was not only Agbarus' half-sister but one of the wives in his extensive harem as well—as his alleged "sister" too, perhaps his favorite "wife'. This is also to some extent the way Sarah—who is supposed to have come from the same area—is portrayed 2,000 years before in the Abraham cycle of stories in Genesis.

The problem in all these sources have to do with names and their translations from one language to another, as for instance, "Bazeus" and "Monobazus", both listed as Helen's husband in Josephus vs. "Abgar" or "Agbarus" in Latin, Greek, Syriac sources. The same problem exists in the New Testament, where "Peter" is sometimes called "Cephas," sometimes "Simon," and sometimes "Sirneon" as he is in "the Jerusalem Council" in Acts 15 we shall refer to below; or characters like "Silas" sometimes perhaps "Silvanus", "Titus" sometimes even perhaps "Timothy" (here Greek vs. Latin usages are the determinant), "Didyrnus" a synonym in Greek for the Aramaic "Thomas," etc., etc.

In his *Geography*, Strabo of Cappadocia makes it clear that the original name of "Edessa" was "Antioch", a claim reflected in Pliny's works in the next century. The problem was that the founder of the Seleucid Empire (if one can call it this), Seleucus, was very enamored of his father named "Antiochus" and therefore named almost every city he founded after him—in the end there were at least four of these! The only way we have to distinguish them is to use a secondary name such as Acts' Antioch in Pisidia or the normal Antioch—on the Orontes—as opposed to Antioch by Callirhoe or Assyrian Antioch (i.e., our "Edessa")—even Antiochia Charax on the lower Tigris, also called Charax Spasini (Basrah), where Queen Helen's son Izates is exiled when he originally encounters the curious character Acts, Josephus, and Eusebius all call "Ananias." In Acts, of course, this curious "Ananias" is carrying on his work in another Syrian locale, "Damascus", when he initially makes the acquaintance of Paul—"on a street called the Straight" no less—at the time of Paul's rather fantastic "conversion," which brings us back to the original topic of this article—"Damascus."

Before this, however, one should look at one more important reference, overlooked by most scholars, "re-erecting the Fallen Tent of David" from Amos 9:11, which is referred to in Column VII of the Damascus Document where "the Star" or "Messianic Prophecy" is also quoted, but familiar from the speech James is pictured as making at the so-called "Jerusalem Council" in Acts 15 before sending his representatives—including Judas Barsabas. Silas, Barnabas, and Paul—down to "Antioch" again with his "Judgments" or determinations. The key is always to determine which "Antioch" one is talking about—the relatively minor and inconsequential one "on the Orontes" in the First Century or, where early Christian (and Jewish) conversion episodes occurred, the one "on the Euphrates by Callirhoe."

For Acts 11:26 earlier, it was here that Christians "were first called Christians", a paradigmatic early Christian, Northern Syrian conversion story if there ever was one. The only question is which "Antioch" we are to understand this is, since the narrator of Acts represents it at this point as the center of a band of Paulinists that even includes someone from the Herodian Royal Family itself—it calls this person "Manean", again probably a garbled version of "Ananias"—and a place from where Paul was said to have set out from with Barnabas for Jerusalem with "famine relief" supplies (c. 44 CE). It should also be appreciated that the thing which triggers Acts' presentation of this celebrated "Jerusalem Council" is that some representatives (clearly "from James" and what Paul calls his "Party of the Circumcision") came down to "Antioch" and taught the brothers that "unless you were circumcised you could not be saved" (Acts 15:1). Again "circumcision" is the issue.

To my knowledge, there are only two other texts which stress this Biblical allusion from Amos 9:11 about "rebuilding the fallen tent of David." They are the Damascus Document from Qumran in the materials following the elucidation of the meaning of "the New Covenant in the Land of Damascus" in Column VI and the curious document from Qumran known as "the *Florilegium*", so—named by John Allegro, a compendium of Messianic allusions much like 2 Corinthians 6:14–7:1. The *Florilegium* interprets this passage in fairly straight-forward Messianic terms, applying it apparently to "the Branch of David", "who will stand" or "arise in the Last Days in Zion to deliver" or "save Israel" (interestingly, the usage here is "*lehoshi'a*," not the usual "*lehazil*"/"to save" of the Habakkuk *Pesher* and elsewhere). But in the *Florilegium*, attached to this individual is another who also makes a key appearance in a pivotal section of the Damascus Document, called "the Interpreter of the *Torah*."

This is not the only usage in this curious compendium of seeming proof texts with language paralleling the Damascus Document—identifying it as part of a cluster probably written about the same time. There are also "the Sons of Zadock" the mention of the Prophet Ezekiel, the use of the terminology "the Last Days" as well as the terminology "*'amod*"/"stand" or "arise" (this can often mean "be resurrected" as well as "stand up") used in connection with "the Branch of David"—in the Damascus Document it comes amid evocation of "the Messiah of Aaron and Israel" (*n.b.*, this allusion is definitely singular here). There is also the usage "cause them to stumble"/"cause them to fall"/or "cast them down" (*hamachshilim/lehachshil*), repeated twice—here specifically denoting "destroying them" and tied to what "Belial" (in Islam "*Iblis*") intended to do to "the Sons of Light."

This usage also forms a key aspect of a passage in the Habakkuk *Pesher* describing what the Wicked Priest did to the Righteous Teacher and those of his persuasion on Yom *Kippur*— "cast them down" (Columns XI–XII), the usage "to destroy them" also appearing in this section about what the Wicked Priests also did to "the Poor" (i.e. "the *Ebionim*" or "*Ebionites*"), seemingly denoting the followers of "the Righteous Teacher." I should not have to add—but I will—this usage "casting down" in Greek forms the central thrust of all descriptions of the death of James in all early Church accounts, most based on the now lost 2nd Century writer Hegesippus, to the attack by "the Enemy" Paul on him in the Pseudoclementine *Recognitions*. Of course, in these same early Church accounts, James' followers were likewise known as "the Poor." Just the fact of the presence of this pivotal allusion to "re- erecting the Fallen Tent of David" here and its similar, if somewhat tendentious, presence in Acts 15's speech attributed to James is fundamental.

But it is to its usage in the crucial passages in the Damascus Document we must turn to get some indication of how all of these conceptualities are being used. In the Damascus Document, paralleling a description first developed in the exegesis of Ezekiel 44:15 about how "the Priests", defined as "the Penitents of Israel", and the "*Nilvim*" or "Joiners with them" in Column IV "went out from the Land of Judah" (probably what we should have to call "Judea"); in familiar passages in Column VI, in exegesis of an archaic "Song" embedded in the text of Numbers 21:18 about "the Lord giving the people water in the wilderness" and the people singing a welcome "Song" about "singing to the well" which "the Princes dug, which the Nobles of the People dug with the Staff'; this time "the Diggers of the People" are defined -just as "the Priests" in Column IV's exegesis of Ezekiel 44: 15 preceding it—as "the Penitents of Israel who went out from the Land of Judah" and the additional passage is added "to dwell" or "sojourn in the Land of Damascus."

This re-elaboration then, properly speaking and taken in its overt sense, constitutes our first reference to "the Syrian Heartland." It is interesting that since the word "*mehokkek*" "staff' also can be interpreted as including a play of the term "hok" or "*hukkim*"/"Laws", "ordinances", or "decrees" in Hebrew; the "Staff' in the exegesis which follows is interpreted as being "the Interpreter of the *Torah*", whom we have already encountered and connected with the "fallen Tent of David" exegesis in the *Florilegium* above. There ,it will be remembered, he is paired with "the Branch of David who will arise to save Israel at the End of Days." In turn, this "Interpreter of the *Torah*" is directly described in terms of Isaiah 54:16's God's having "created an instrument for His works." In this instance, we are obviously talking about Divine "works", in the sense of God's Holy plan.

Whereas the overt meaning of the passage in Isaiah 54:26 is that of a "weapon" being created by the "Smith" (meaning, of course, God or the Lord) to destroy any weapon being used against the subjects of the poem, identified as the Servants "established in Righteousness" (54: 14), who "do Righteousness" and "keep Judgment" (56:1) and "love the Name of the Lord" (56:6). This passage, which in Isaiah as we saw is a "Song", following directly on or, if one prefers, continuing—for continuing it surely does—the famous "Suffering Servant" materials in Isaiah 53 and the basis of all "Christian" exegesis that subsequently is to develop; closes in Isaiah 56:3 and 6 with an ecstatic evocation of these same "*Nilvim*"/"Joiners" just encountered above in Column IV of the Damascus Document in exegesis of Ezekiel 44:15; but here it is clear these are "foreigners who have joined themselves to the Lord", i.e., once again, these same "Joiners."

As long as these "keep the Sabbath, choosing what pleases (Him), and hold fast to the Covenant"—language found in the closing exhortations of the Damascus Document ("all those that hold fast to the Statutes, coming and going according to the *Torah* and listening to the voice of the Teacher"/"Moreh"—CD XX.27–28); these will also be found acceptable in the Temple and added to those "already gathered" there (Isaiah 56:8). Throughout my work for over three and a half decades, I have always insisted that these "*Nilvim*", mentioned in the Damascus Document's exposition of Ezekiel 44:15, were "Gentile converts attaching themselves to the Community" or to "God." Here one finds further confirmation of this proposition in these above-cited passages from Isaiah, all of which reflect the mind set of those composing these documents.

For the Damascus Document, therefore, this "*Mehokkek*" or "*Doresh*"/Interpreter "decrees (*hakak*) the on going on ordinances" (here "*Mehokkekot*"/"the staves" or "ordinance", playing on the obvious parallel—but note too the intense alliteration going on here as well) with which "the Princes and the Nobles of the People dug the well" and "in which they should walk until the Standing up (also possibly "Resurrection" here) of the One who Pours down Righteousness (*Yoreh-Zedek* —another play, this time on *Moreh-Zedek* or "the Righteous Teacher") at the End of Days" (CD VI.6–11). Though the imagery here is admittedly complex while at the same time manifestly beautiful, the thrust should be readily clear. Here "the Penitents of Israel" are identical to "the Diggers" and they parallel "the Priests" in the earlier exegesis of Column IV. Here, too, the seeming redundancy represented by the phrase "the Nobles of the People" are probably to be identified with "the *Nilvim*" or "Joiners" of the first exegesis, the connecting piece being the allusion to "People" or "Peoples"—once again to be taken in the sense of and meaning obviously in this case "Gentiles."

These are the ones who apply the ordinances or "staves" and so the imagery of "the Well of Living Waters," picked up later in the narrative in Column VIII, where "the New Covenant in the Land of Damascus" is being elucidated, is complete. The reason all of these are attached to the all-important phraseology from Isaiah 54—56 is that this too is presented as part of a "Song" or "Singing"$_{I}$ (54:1), "the Song" or "Singing" of an old classical piece being evoked from Numbers 21:18. But the elucidation at this point in the text of "Princes" is slightly different than that of "Nobles" and one must always be cognizant of these slight variations even if perhaps a bit a redundant. It would appear that "the Interpreter" or "the *Doresh*"/"the Seeker" is to be included within the category of "the Princes", because they too are described as "seeking God" (CD V1.6). "The Staff" or "Doresh decrees the Laws" or "Staves" and it is with these that "the Nobles of the People" dig the well—very obscure, but splendidly breathtaking imagery.

The whole tenor of this section from Isaiah should also be noted as one directed to "the barren that did not bear", "the sons of the forsaken one being no less than the married"/"the ashamed"/"the confounded"/"the cast-off wife of the youth for a moment forsaken." In fact, the whole passage is actually speaking of ultimate hopefulness even in the face of the great tragedy that appears to be unfolding. This is the same kind of feeling one gets in the last phrases of the Habakkuk *Pesher* in Column XII–XIII. It should be understood and appreciated that the sense is the same which, once more, points to a common chronological milieu of national tragedy, but not of either forsakenness or hopelessness.

As the Damascus Document proceeds into its climactic final description of "the New Covenant in the Land of Damascus" and the "Re-erecting" there of "the fallen Tent of David", it process through allusions to "doing according to the precise letter of the *Torah*" and uses the "Nazirite"-style language of "*lihinazzer*" and "*lehazzir*" (VI.15 and VII.1). A third such evocation comes in VIII.8 and is used to describe how one is supposed "to separate from the Sons of the Pit" and "keep way from "polluted evil Riches", including "the Riches of the Temple" (in this context and at this time, presumably polluted by Herodian and Roman contributions—VI.14–16, if we are to see these allusions as relating to the Post-Maccabean Period as the author does) and "to distinguish between Holy and profane" (the very opposite of what Peter is taught to do a vengeful, war-like Messiah as in the War Scroll—"the rest will be given over to the avenging sword of the Covenant."

Again too, there is little doubt of the tragicness of the times. For Manuscript A, which is more detailed, this "Messiah" is "the Star who shall go forth from Jacob, the Scepter that shall rise from Israel" (Numbers 24:17, i.e., "the Star Prophecy" again), with whose "standing up" or "arising, "all the Sons of Seth" (this from the original in Numbers 24:17) would be destroyed. Here, once again, it would appear that the Messiah comes to destroy primarily Gentiles not necessarily Jews, a Messiah of the cut of "Simon bar Kochba"/"the Son of the Star." For

Column VIII.2, this same "Judgment" will be upon those who "entered the Covenant, but did not hold fast to these Laws" and "Statutes" (again the "steadfastness" imagery). They would be destroyed by "the hand of Belial" ("Iblis" again)—in this instance, most certainly the "'Herodians" together with their sponsors, the Romans.

This Messiah is actually referred to as the "*Nasi chol ha-'Edah*", a term known to have been used by Bar Kochba on his coinage and familiar from an assortment of other Qumran documents (or instance, in the famous Fragment 4Q285 containing allusion to "woundings", "*Nasi chol ha- Edah*" is identified with "the Branch of David, the Shoot of Jesse"—of course all familiar and famous "Messianic" language). But in this all-important *Pesher* on "the fallen Tent of David", "the Star" is actually "the Interpreter of the *Torah* who came to Damascus", passages which seem to have an odd, but inverted parallel in the Book of Acts as it has come down to us. Here "the *Doresh*" or "Interpreter" actually assumes Messianic proportions for what he appears to be achieving at Damascus or in the wilderness thereof. It is hard to say this about the "Paul" in Acts who comes to Damascus and is pictured as arguing with everyone.

But to return to the escapees, who are compared to the Ephraimites escaping from the Judeans (VII. 12–13—in the Nahum *Pesher*, for instance, "the Simple of Ephraim" would again appear to be a euphemism for Gentiles or at least, what in other contexts might go by the name of "Samaritans." That *Pesher* wants them to once more return to the path of "Righteousness")—again our omnipresent "Steadfast Ones" appear (*ha-Mahzakim*). Here the basis of the exegesis are these famous passages from Amos 5:26–27 and 9:11 about "exiling the Tabernacle of the King" and "resurrecting the Fallen Tent of David" from Amos 9:11. In the way these passages are put together, it begins to appear that we must look to a land even further North than Damascus for the focus of a good deal of this activity and interest.

Not only are we speaking about escaping to "the Land of the North", which would clearly appear to hark back to the earlier Exile under the Assyrians in the 700s BCE; but the way these quotations from Amos are being parsed, all the words are being deconstructed and taken separately, though the whole is being interpreted in a clearly "Messianic" way, as its connection with "the Star Prophecy from Numbers 24:17 to follow irrefutably proves. Needless to say the exposition is arcane and extremely obscure, but "the King" (as per Pauline exposition of Jesus in 1 Corinthians) is definitely stated to by "the Community", but "the Tabernacle of the King," in an esoteric exposition of immense import is definitely said to be "the Books of the Law." For these purposes, "the Bases of the Statues", also referred to in Amos 5:27, are "the Books of the Prophets, whose words Israel" is said "to have rejected."

Of course, even the original in Amos is arcane and, though the Damascus Document struggles to render it intelligible, in the end it does not do succeed in doing so at least for the modem reader. The only real sense that can be made out of it, other than a completely esoteric meaning, is the implication that something -presumably "the Tent of David"—is being "exiled beyond Damascus" or, as it were, to "the Land North of Damascus"—for our purposes, of course, "Northern Syria." Finally all these things are being connected in some manner with the "re-erecting' or "establishing of the Fallen Tent of David" which follows, seemingly meant to expound the whole, then proceeding to evoke the Messianic "Interpreter of the Law" and "Nasi" material centering around the "Damascus" allusions again. So, however one interprets them, we are in a "Damascus" milieu and surrounding allusions about "the Tent being exiled North from Damascus" seem to point to a Land even further North in Northern Syria. I think we can explain these in terms of the conversions we cited at the beginning of King Agbarus/Abgarus, "the King of the Peoples beyond the Eurphrates, Queen Helen and her sons, and even Paul's and his sometime colleague "Ananias"'s somewhat questionable activities there. These passages from Ms. A sf the Damascus Document are extent at Qumran (4Q266, Fr. 3, Column 2), though the more cursory parallels represented by the variation in Fragment B have not so far been paralleled.

Before moving on to how these things may or may not link up with events being described in Acts "North of Damascus", it would behoove one to just briefly deal with the parallels represented by the "Letter" or "Letters" called now by all scholars after the reconstruction in the 1980's *MMT* ("Some Words of the *Torah*") In the first place, almost everyone agrees that this "Letter"—the only one of its kind so far extant at Qumran and this in multiple copies, which testify to its importance—is addressed to a "King" of some kind. This is made clear by the reference in the Second Part of the reconstructed text to the King's "own good and that of his People" (what "People"—that is the key), recapitulated in line 33 of the Second Part with the evocation of the words the Bible applies to Abraham in Genesis 16, "being reckoned to you as Righteousness" so familiar to anyone knowledgeable about "Christian" theology, since they are part of the whole "being reckoned to you as Righteousness" debate, whether in Paul's Romans, Galatians, Hebrews, or in James, as we publicly pointed out from the first moment the Document was made public.

The idea of referring to this King's "People" almost makes it look as if they are distinct or a foreign people to those writing the "Letter"—as just pointed out, the only such document found at Qumran and, in my view, a "Jamesian" one. To accept this would of course be momentous, though this is not a provable implication or suggestion is there. Not only does this Second Section refer repeatedly to "the Book of Moses", i.e., and "the words of the Prophets" (Lines 6, 10, 11, 16, 24, etc.) seemingly recapitulating the words of the exegesis above in Ms. A of the Damascus Document that "the Tabernacle of the King is the Books of the *Torah*" and "the bases of the statues are the Books of the Prophets"—again, in this manner, firming up the connection between these two document—but it also refers to and "the End Time" (13, 15, 24, 33), further strengthening the parallels and, as a consequence, the connections. Moreover, the whole framework of mentioning Jereboam and Zedekiah in the text is similar to the framework of alluding either Assyrian or Babylonian times in these parallel passages in CD.

But, in addition, the interest this "King" obviously appears to have in the Letter(s) in David, who is reckoned as "a man of pious (works). . .saved from many sufferings and forgiven" (Lines 28–29), parallels the interest in David both in these "re-erecting the fallen Tent of David" passages in CD VII, but a not to mention in the *Florilegium* already remarked. Even the words one finds in Line 5 of the Second Section of *MMT,* "never to turn back", have a ringing parallel in the fulsome condemnations of those who "turn back and betray the Well of further descriptions of "the New Covenant in the Land of Damascus" in CD VII.22ff. and Ms. B XX.1ff.

In fact, even in the First Section of the reconstructed text of *MMT,* if one looks at the regulations, most of which as announced in the first Lines 3–4 of the Letter itself, having to do with gifts—primarily Gentile gifts—to the Temple and, as a consequence, purity regulations related to these, that is, in particular, the purity of the Temple. This, of course, is once again a subject of concern to Columns IV–VIII of the Damascus Document and, most significantly, perhaps the main concern along with "fornication" of the "Third of Belial's Nets" announced in CD V, "the pollution of the Temple." Furthermore, one can immediately see that these generally break down roughly into the areas of James' directives to overseas communities—no matter how they re-parsed in Paul's 1 Corinthians 8–12—which follow directly upon James' own actually—quoted evocation of "re-erecting the Fallen Tent of David" in the speech attributed to him in Acts 15:7, that is, "abstain" or "keep away from (even this language is replicated in the "Nazirite" language of the passages from CD, cited above and having to do with *lehinnazer/lehazzir"*, i.e., "keeping way from things sacrificed to idols, fornication, blood, and strangled things" (by way of an aside and a parallel interest, also of concern to the Koran!).

In fact, one could almost view *MMT* as a not very systematic midrash or exposition of these categories, in particular "things sacrificed to idols" which Paul so fulminates against from 1 Corinthians 8–12, as we just said, ending up with its mirror opposite "consuming the body and blood of Christ Jesus". In fact, the whole issue of "Gentile gifts in the Temple", particularly significant for Gentile converts and "the Gentile Mission" per se. For instance, in regard to this category of "things sacrificed to an idol," the statement is made that "it is the idol that seduces them" which is actually almost directly responded to by Paul himself in   Corinthians 8:4: "We know that an idol has no real existence[1]", followed by approximately eight lines of like-minded analysis and dissimulation. But it should also be observed that Josephus himself testifies in his Jewish War that this was the issue that started the War against Rome, when the daily sacrifices on behalf of the Emperor were stopped; but not only this, when such sacrifices by or on behalf of Gentiles were rejected by the now "Revolutionary" Priesthood in the Temple, a thing he observes "our Forefathers used to accept", but which is also a concern throughout the early lines of *MMT*!

The issue of "fornication" is also taken up in *MMT* from Line 47 onwards, focusing particularly on mixed marriages. "Mixed" marriages are specifically banned in Lines 47–59, particularly where "Holy Persons" were concerned, seemingly meaning here Priests, an viewed itself as an entire "Community of Holy Ones (Lines 85–89). Lines 83 and 89 actually mention "fornication" and the ban on it, reflected not only James but also material throughout the Damascus Document and, one might add, the Temple Scroll.

Since the issue of "strangled things" in Acts' rather garbled version of James' directives to overseas communities can be directly comprehended as "carrion," which is of course the sense given it in the Pseudoclementines and, thereafter, in the Koran; this too is directly touched upon in the passage "banning the bringing of dogs into the Holy Camp," i.e., Jerusalem, "because they might eat the bones with the flesh still on them" (Lines 66–70). The ban on "blood," while not specifically mentioned per se can, of course, be thought of as operative throughout.

If one now attempts a reconstruction based on Acts' handling of similar materials, in particular, those coming in the more reliable last third and particularly the "we" materials, following directly in Chapter 16 upon the only a little less reliable "Jerusalem Council" portrait in 15. Where this so-called "Jerusalem Council" is concerned, we have already mentioned the issue of "Antioch" when we began this essay. For the purposes of Northern Syrian renderings, its precise location really wouldn't matter; but for the purposes of the argument, let us assume it was the more substantial one in First Century CE terms, that is, "Antioch by Callirhoe" or the one on "on the Euphrates" where "the King of the Edessenes" held sway. Then Agbarus' Kingdom in Northern Syria and its extension in his marital relations with Queen Helen's (whether she was also his sister or not, as Armenian and Syriac sources insist) and that of her two sons further East can be thought of as the focus of where Paul's initial "Christian" "Missionary" activities took place and where his original "Christian Community," according to Acts, was located.

This too would consolidate the activities of Josephus' "Ananias", prominent both in Acts version of Paul's activities in "Damascus" as we saw, but also mentioned as the intermediary with King Agbams in Eusebius' presentation of a messenger from Jerusalem to this King, into a single Northern Syrian context. The same for both Queen Helen's and Paul and Barnabas' well-advertised famine relief activities in both Christian and Jewish sources—according to Josephus and seemingly in Acts in the mid-40s CE and a subject we have treated at length in *James the Brother of Jesus,* Penguin, 1998. This is true regardless of what one considered the exact relationship of Helen, "Bazeus" (seemingly a garbled version of "Monobazus" in Josephus), Izates, and Agbarus ("Agbarus" and "Monobazus" probably parallel titles in different linguistic frameworks anyhow) to be. We have also already signaled the importance of the issue of "circumcision" in Josephus' description (backed up too by the *Talmud)* of Izates' conversion, as it is in Acts' account of what scholars denote as "the Jerusalem Council" (not to mention the veiled contemptuous parody in the thrust of Acts' "Ethiopian Queen's eunuch" materials earlier following its picture of "Paul and Barnabas" famine-relief activities), Paul's letters, and the Damascus Document's presentation of Abraham. The Ammonite/Moabite issue, not unrelated to it, is also mentioned both in *MMT* and the *Florilegium,* both of which have a central focus on David as well as we have seen.

Putting all these materials together, it is possible to consider "*MMT*" as the letter brought down by Judas Barsabas and Silas, which Acts claims was addressed to "the brothers who are of the Gentiles in Antioch (Edessa by Callirhoe and beyond) and Syria and Cilicia" (15:23), not to mention the "letters" Eusebius claims were delivered to a King there and, for him, perhaps the first conversion to what he is calling "Christianity." Setting aside what Acts considers to be the upshot of the so-called "Jerusalem Council" and James' "rulings" there, "rulings" very much in the character of the powers accorded "the *Mebakker*" or "Overseer" (in Christianity, "Bishop") at Qumran and described in detail in closing Columns of the Damascus Document; it is possible now to actually turn to the content of it and both the *Florilegium* and the Damascus Document's evocation of "the Re-erection of the Fallen Tent of David."

Acts' presentation of this image in James' speech—no introduction of whom this particular "James" might be, since the other James had already supposedly been executed—is preceded by words also attributed to James, in which he relates how "Simeon (is this "Peter.' or could it be with even more logic, "Simeon bar Cleophas", since "Peter" has already supposedly fled the country with a death sentence on his head five chapters earlier?) has related how *God first visited the Gentiles* to take out of them a People for His Name" (italics mine). In this picture, James then goes on to quote, as in *MMT*, "the words of the Prophets." The shift here from "Books of the Prophets" as in CD VII to "words of the Prophets" as in *MMT* is surely not insignificant. But even more so is James' use of the expression "visited" just highlighted. Used in this manner, it is almost exclusively a usage known to the Damascus Document, occurring throughout from the description of how God *"visited them and caused a Root of Planting to grow out of Aaron and Israel"* (italics again mine) in the very First Column, to repeated evocations of "visiting their works" (with Wrath) in V.16, to the "Era of the First Visitation" of Column VII.21, and finally to the "Visitation" of "Judgment on all those who entered His Covenant; who did not remain steadfast" to the Law, which is also described as "the Day in which God visits" or "commands" in CD VIII.2–3. These correspondences are so unique that they appear to approach irrefutability.

However this may be, as James is presented as using this term in Acts, it is a "Visitation" for goodness or reward, the operative terms in all renderings being "People" or "Peoples" in Greek as well as Hebrew—"Peoples" generally being the Qumran term for Gentiles, as it is, for instance, in Eusebius' rendering of Agbarus' title "the Great King of the Peoples beyond the Euphrates", as we saw and meaning both the Land of the Edessenes and Adiabene and beyond—areas to which inter alia Josephus appears to have first addressed his Aramaic and original version of *The Jewish War.*

Though the general rendering here is closer to the Septuagint version of the passage than the Masoretic, still the operative words, even as they appear in Amos 9:12, are "Gentiles"—*Greek Ethnon.* This is clearly why they are being evoked here in Acts, because what is ostensibly being debated is "Gentiles" and how to treat them or, more specifically, Paul's "Gentile Mission." But it is also important because James uses it in conjunction with the Damascus Document's allusion "re-erecting the Fallen Tent of David." Here too "called by My Name" is also evoked, an expression familiar throughout the whole of Acts, where normally it is applied to Jesus rather than God. This too has a variant in the all-important exegesis of Ezekiel 44:15 in the Damascus Document, "called by Name", specifically applied to "the Sons of Zadok" in Column IV.

For *MMT,* too, the issue is Gentiles but, of course, the outcome is quite different than Acts' presents it or alleges, if the parallel is allowed. In the *Florilegium,* the passage is once again applied to those "who turn aside from the path of Evil", seemingly identified once again with "Gentiles" and "their idols" and, as in *MMT* and the Damascus Document, the time is that of "the Last Days." Once again "the Sons of Zadok" are evoked, but the exegesis, as we saw at the start, is the straightforward one to "the Branch of David" and/or "the Interpreter of the Law" and the presentation is definitely applied to a Bar Kochba-like Messianic Saviour.

Though in the Damascus Document, the thrust is similar, if

more esoteric, and does some to be aimed either at the Syrian hinterland or an area North of there as we have explained; there are limitations of an application to "Righteous" Gentiles observing the Law as well as Jews, particularly in its final passages, where an exhortation occurs in which what the Letter of James in the New Testament calls "the Royal Law according to the Scripture" together with is concomitant "fortifying" language are once more evoked XX.18–19). Here the operative words are: "a Book of Remembrances before Him (God) for God-Fearers and those reckoning His Name" (XX.1 9–20).

Of course, the relationship to Jesus' alleged words at "the Last Supper," "do" or "drink this in Remembrance of me" should not be overlooked. Again, it is clear that these words at the very end of the Damascus Document apply to Gentiles, as they do presumably in the Gospels' version of these words of attributed to the "Jesus" they are portraying) and the parallel with James' speech in Acts again becomes tangible. All these parallels are further reinforced by the language in the very next clause: "Until God shall reveal Salvation (*Yesha'*—if one likes "Jesus") and Righteousness" or "Justification to those fearing His Name" —i.e., again "the God—Fearers", Jewish, Gentile, or even Muslims to come.

Here is the powerful parallel to Amos 9:11–12's "and all the Gentiles who are called by My Name", loosely quoted by James in Acts 15: 17 and James' actually quoted variation of this: "how God first visited the Gentiles to take out of them a People for His Name" in the same speech. This language of "strengthening" and emphasis on God's Holy "Name" continues to the end of the Damascus Document, as we just savy, declaring as does *MMT*, that "all those who hold fast to these statutes, coming and going in according with the Law (XX.27–28) and have not lifted up (their) hand against the Holiness of His Laws and the Righteousness of His Judgments. . . and not deserted the Laws of Righteousness. . .; their heart(s) shall be strengthened and they shall prevail against all the Sons of Earth" (here, the ethos parallels the Qumran War Scroll again). . . and they *shall see His Salvation* (i.e., "*Yeshu'a*"), because *they took refuge in His Holy Name*" (italics mine).

This seems to me to be the gist both of James' evocation of the "re-erecting the Fallen Tent of David" passage in Acts and the same words in the Damascus Document at Qumran. It is for these reasons as well that we consider both the conversion of "King Agbarus" in 'Christian' tradition and Helen's household in 'Jewish'—in Eusebius' rendering, one follows the other—relevant to the whole sense of both these passages in CD and the instructions on the subject of "Gentile gifts in the Temple" (in other words, "things sacrificed to an idol") and "fornication" in *MMT*. The veiled allusions in both documents to David and ultimately Abraham just adds further weight to this conclusion. As I see it, all these references converge and are pointed towards events, we can now only dimly make out or perceive, but with the use of a little intelligent historical analysis, they can be gingerly teased from the existing data, much as DNA can be teased from long-discarded human remains. It all depends both on one's discernment and one's insight.

BIBLIOGRAPHY

Achtemeier, P., *The Quest for Unity in the New Testament* Church, Fortress, Philadelphia, 1987.

Alon, G., *The Jews in their Land in the Talmudic Age*, Cambridge, 1994.

Bainton, R. H., *Early Christianity*, New York, 1960.

Balch, D., (ed.), *Social History of the Matthean Community*, Fortress, Minneapolis, 1991.

Bauckharn, R., (ed.), *The Book of Acts in its Palestinian Setting*, Grand Rapids, 1995.

Baumgarten, J., *DJD XVII: The Damascus Document*, Oxford, 1996.

Bell, H. I., *Jews and Christians In Egypt*, London, 1924.

Berger, K., *Qumran und Jesus*, Stuttgart, 1993.

Betz, and R. Reisner, *Jesus, Qumran, and the Vatican*, New York, 1994

Black, C. C., *Paul and Qumran: Studies in New Testament Exegesis*, Chicago, 1968.

Brandon, S. G. F., *Jesus and the Zealots*, London, 1967.

Brooke, G., *New Qumran Texts and Studies*, Leiden, 1995.

Brooke, G., *Temple Scroll Studies*, Sheffield, 1989.

Brown, R. E., *The Community of the Beloved Disciple*, New York, 1979.

Brown, S., *The Origins of Christianity: A Historical Introduction into the New Testament*, Oxford, 1993.

Bruce, F. F., *New Testament History, revised ed.*, New York, 1971.

Bruce F. F., *Peter, Stephen, James and John: Studies in Non-Pauline Christianity*, Grand Rapids, 1980.

Bultmann R., *Primitive Christianity in its Contemporary Setting*, New York, 1956.

Bultmann, R., *Theology of the New Testament*, New York, 1951.

Charlesworth, J., *Jesus and the Dead Sea Scrolls*, New York, 1993.

Charlesworth, J., *John and the Dead Sea Scrolls*, New York, 1990.

Charlesworth, J., *The Messiah: Developments in Earliest Christianity*,

Minneapolis, 1992.

Cohen, S., *From the Maccabees to the Mishnah,* Philadelphia, 1987.

Collins, J. J., *The Apocalyptic Imagination,* New York, 1992. Cook, E., *Solving the Mysteries of the Dead Sea Scrolls: New Light on the Bible,* Grand Rapids, 1994.

Cross F. M., *The Ancient Library at Qumran and Modern Biblical Study,* Grand Rapids, 1980.

Crossan, J. D., *The Historical Jesus: The Life of a Mediterranean Jewish*

Peasant, San Francisco, 1991.

Cullmann, *Peter: Disciple, Apostle, and Martyr,* London, 1953.

Danielou, J., *Theologie du Judeo-Chistianisme, Journal,*

Danielou, J., *Gospel Message and Hellenistic Culture,* Philadelphia, 1973.

Davies, W.D., *The Setting of the Sermon on the Mount,* London, 1963.

Dibelius, M. and Greeven, H., *James: A Commentary on the Epistle of James,* Philadelphia, 1976.

Dibelius M. and Kummel, W. G., *Paul,* Philadelphia, 1957.

Dominic, J,. *Who Killed Jesus? Exposing the Roots of Anti-Semitism In the Gospel Story of the Death of Jesus,* San Francisco, 1995.

Eisenman, R., *The Dead Sea Scrolls and the First Christians: Essays and Translations, Harper Collins,* London, 1996.

Eisenman, R., and Robinson, J., *A Facsimile Edition of the Dead Sea Scrolls (2 vols.), B.A.S.,* Washington D. C., 1991.

Eisenman, R., and Wise, M., *The Dead Sea Scrolls Uncovered, PB, Penguin, New York,* 1993.

Eisenman, R., *James the Brother of Jesus: The Key to Unlocking the Secrets of the Dead Sea Scrolls and Early Christianity,* New York, 1997

Eisenman, R., *James the Just in the Habakkuk Pesher,* The Way Publishing, 2019 (most recent edition).

Eisenman, R., *Maccabees, Zedok, Christians and Qumran: A New Hypothesis of Qumran Origins,* The Way Publishing, 2019 (most recent edition).

Eisenman, R., *The New Testament Code: The Cup of the Lord, The Damascus Covenant, and the Blood of Christ,* The Way Publishing, 2019 (most recent edition).

Elliott-Binns, L. E., *Galilean Christianity,* London, 1956.

Enslin, M. S., *Christian Beginnings, 2 vols.,* New York, 1956.

Feldman, L., *Jew and Gentile in the Ancient Vorld,* Princeton, 1993.

Fitzmeyer, J., *The Dead Sea Scrolls: Major Publications and Tools for Study,* Atlanta, 1990.

Fitzmyer, J., *The Scepter and the Star: The Messiahs of the Dead Sea Scrolls and Other Ancient Literature,* 1995.

Flusser, D., *Judaism and the Origins of Christianity,* Jerusalem, 1988.

Garcia-Martinez, F., *The Dead Sea Scrolls Translated,* Leiden, 1994.

Goehring, J., *Gospel Origins and Christian Beginnings,* Sonoma, 1990.

Goodman, M., *The Ruling Class of Judaea: The Origins of the Jewish Revolt against Rome, A.D. 66–70,* Cambridge, 1987.

Goodman, M., *Mission and Conversion: Proselytizing in the Religious History of the Roman Empire,* Oxford, 1994.

Goppelt, L., *Apostolic and Post-Apostolic Times,* New York, 1970.

Hanson, K., *Dead Sea Scrolls: The Untold Story,* New York, 1997.

Harnack, V., *The Mission and Expansion of Christianity in the First Three Centuries, 2 vols,* New York, 1908.

Hemer, C., *The Book of Acts in the Setting of Hellenistic History,* Tubingen, 1989.

Hengel, M., *Between Jesus and Paul,* London, 1983.

Hengel, M., *The Zealots,* Philadelphia, 1989.

Hennecke, E., and Schneemelcher, W., *New Testament Apocrypha, 2 vols,* Philadelphia, 1964–7.

Herford, T. R., *Christianity in Talmud and Midrash,* London, 1903.

Hill, C., *Hellenists and Hebrews: Reappraising Division within the Earliest Church,* Minneapolis, 1992.

Horsley, R., and Silberman, N.A., *The Messiah and the Kingdom: How Jesus and Paul Ignited a Revolution and Transformed the Ancient World,* New York, 1997.

James, M. R., *The Apocryphal New Testament*, Oxford, 1963.

Jeremias, J., *Jerusalem in the Time of Jesus*, Philadelphia, 1969.

Josephus, *The Antiquities, Loeb Edition* (or any popular Edition) *Judaism and Hellenism*, Philadelphia, 1974.

Josephus, *The Jewish War, Loeb Edition (or any popular edition) The Johannine Circle*, Philadelphia, 1976.

Klljn, A., *Patristic Evidence for Jewish-Christian Sects*, Leiden, 1973.

Koester, H., *Ancient Christian Gospels: Their History and Development, Philadelphia, 1995 Ludemann, G., Paul Apostle to the Gentiles: Studies in Chronology*, Philadelphia, 1984.

Luedemann, G., *Earliest Christianity According to the Tradition in Acts*, Minneapolis, 1989.

Maccoby, H., *&thmaker: Paul and the Invention of Christianity*, London, 1986.

Mack, B., *The Lost Gospel: The Book of Q and Christian Origins*, San Francisco, 1993.

Mack, B., *Who Wrote the New Testament? The Making of the Christian Myth*, San Francisco, 1995.

Meeks, W., *The First Urban Christians: The Social World of Paul*, New Haven, 1983.

Meeks, W., (ed.), *The Writings of St. Paul*, New York, 1972.

Mor, M., *The Bar Kochba Revolt: Its Extent and Effect*, Jerusalem, 1991.

Murphy-O'Connor, J., *Paul: A Critical Life*, Oxford, 1996.

Neusner, J., *Judaism in the Beginning of Christianity*, Philadelphia, 1984.

Nickelsburg, G., *Jewish Literature between Bible and the Mishnah*, Philadelphia, 1981.

Nickelsburg, G., *Resurrection, Immortality, and Eternal Life in Intertestamental Judaism*, New York, 1972.

Overman, A., *Matthew's Gospel and Formative Judaism: The Social World of the Matthean Community*, Minneapolis, 1990.

Pagels, E., *The Gnostic Gospels*, New York, 1979.

Richardson, P., *Herod: King of the Jews and Friend of the Romans,* South Carolina, 1996.

Robinson, J. M. (ed.), *The Nag Hammadi Library,* New York, 1977.

Rousseau, J. and Ariv, R., *Jesus and His World, Fortress,* Philadelphia, 1995.

Russell, D. S., *From Early Judaism to Early Church,* Philadelphia, 1986.

Sanders, E. P., *The Historical Figure of Jesus,* Penguin, New York, 1995.

Sanders, E. P., *Jesus and Judaism,* London, 1985.

Sandmel, S., *Judaism and Christian Beginnings,* Oxford, 1978.

Schiffman, L., *Law, Custom, and Messianism in the Dead Sea Sect,* Jerusalem, 1993.

Schiffman, L., *Reclaiming the Dead Sea Scrolls,* Philadelphia, 1994.

Segal, A., *Paul the Convert: The Apostolate and Apostasy of Saul the Pharisee,* New Haven, 1990.

Shanks, H., *Christianity and Rabbinic Judaism: Parallel History of their Origins and Early Development, B.A.S.,* Washington D.C., 1994.

Silberman, N. A., *The Hidden Scrolls,* New York, 1994.

Thiering, B., *Jesus and the Riddle of the Dead Sea Scrolls,* San Francisco, 1992.

VanderKam, J., *The Dead Sea Scrolls Today,* Grand Rapids, 1994.

Wacholder, B. Z. and Abegg, M., *A Preliminary Edition of the Unpublished Dead Sea Scrolls, B.A.S.,* Washington D. C., 1991.

Wachsman, S., *The Sea of Galilee Boat,* New York, 1995.

Wise, M., *A Critical Study of the Temple Scroll from Qumran Cave 11,* Chicago, 1990.

Wise, M., *Thunder in Gemini and Other Essays on the Language and Literature of Second Temple Palestine,* Sheffield, 1994.

Wise, M., Abegg, M., and Cook, E., *The Dead Sea Scrolls: A New Translation,* San Francisco, 1996.

Printed in Dunstable, United Kingdom

75922676R00048